Leading a Life with God

LEADING
a Life
G O D
with

The Practice of
Spiritual Leadership

DANIEL WOLPERT

UPPER
ROOM BOOKS®
NASHVILLE

The Upper Room® Web site: www.upperroom.org

UPPER ROOM®, UPPER ROOM BOOKS® and design logos are trademarks owned by The Upper Room®, Nashville, Tennessee. All rights reserved.

Unless otherwise noted, scripture quotations are from the New Revised Standard Version Bible, copyright 1989 Division of Christian Education of the National Council of the Churches of Christ in the United States of America. Used by permission. All rights reserved. Scripture noted KJV is from the King James Version. Scripture noted AP is Author's Paraphrase.

Cover and interior design: The DesignWorks Group
                                        thedesignworksgroup.com
Cover illustration: Getty Images
First printing: 2006

LIBRARY OF CONGRESS CATALOGING-IN-PUBLICATION DATA
Wolpert, Daniel, 1959–
    Leading a life with God : prayer practices for spiritual leaders /by Daniel Wolpert.
        p. cm.
    ISBN 13-digit: 978-0-8358-1003-6
    ISBN 10-digit: 0-8358-1003-8
    1. Prayer—Christianity. 2. Christian leadership. 3. Leadership—Religious aspects—Christianity. I. Title.
    BV210.3.W65 2006
    248.3'2—dc22   2006008616

Printed in the United States of America

*To my friends at the First Presbyterian Church
of Crookston, Minnesota,
fellow Christians who every day teach me
about leading a life with God.*

CONTENTS

INTRODUCTION

*M*y first book, *Creating a Life with God: The Call of Ancient Prayer Practices*, had several goals. First, I wanted to present prayer practices and how to do them. Second, I wanted to situate these practices within the context of the church and lift them up as a vibrant part of our spiritual history—not something we are borrowing from the Buddhists! Finally, I attempted to place these practices in a framework to demonstrate their relevance not as isolated activities but rather as components of a spiritual life, a life in Christ. As disciples and followers of Jesus, we are called to live out such a life in this world. All these tasks were undertaken from the point of view of the individual—or a group of individuals—interested in partaking of the life of prayer—the spiritual life.

From my perspective as a pastor and a student of the life of prayer for twenty-five years, the goals of *Creating a Life with God* are the necessary first steps for someone or a group of people in community who want to pray in a deeper way. This book, *Leading a Life with God,* addresses the next requirement for deepening a community's spiritual life, namely spiritual leadership.

Two thousand years ago, a small group of people went out from an upper room to create a new faith (Acts 1:13–2:47). As far as we know, they had little education, no programs, no curricula, no denominational certification. But they did have one thing: the power of the Spirit. And it was through that Spirit that they were able to lead and do the work God was calling them to; God, through their faithful prayer lives, transformed them into spiritual leaders.

God wants the fruits of prayer and the gospel to be spread to the entire world. This transmission occurs as people involved in the spiritual life are called to help others along this journey. I have met hundreds of individuals who, like the early disciples, feel called to guide others to a deeper relationship with Jesus. But I have also encountered the difficulty in making a transition from praying alone or as a participant in a group to leading a group or organization in prayer. That shift appears to be quite challenging. One can pray the practices outlined in *Creating a Life with God* for years yet still struggle mightily when it comes time to introduce these practices into churches or other groups.

Currently "spiritual leadership" is a very hot topic. In preparing this book I've read many of the best-selling resources on the subject. I consistently find that these books provide insights from secular leadership disciplines and then add a paragraph or two about how all these disciplines should be "led by the Spirit." I have yet to find a resource describing in depth *how to be led by the Spirit.* Such a description is the purpose of this volume.

I have revisited the twelve chapters of *Creating a Life with God* with an eye toward spiritual leadership. Thus each topic and each set of prayer practices are linked to an aspect of spiritual leadership. I describe this aspect in depth, discuss how to use and apply it in church situations, and show how each leadership piece fits together with the life of prayer. Another aim of the book is to clarify how personal practice evolves into leadership practice.

Because this book concerns leadership arising out of the practice of prayer, I do assume some familiarity with the contemplative life and prayer practices. However, I also hope to encourage some who do not have this familiarity to begin praying. Luckily there are now many wonderful books on prayer and how to pray available, which can be used in conjunction with this one. In addition, the appendix explains the how-to of several prayer techniques. Practices described in the appendix appear in SMALL CAPITAL letters in the text.

As in *Creating a Life with God*, a "traveling companion" accompanies each chapter. These traveling companions provide images of persons who use the prayer practices in their lives. All the traveling companions in this book are biblical figures, which grounds the practice of spiritual leadership in the scriptures that guide the life of faith.

My passion for *Creating a Life with God* came from my own experience in the life of prayer. I have a similar sense of passion for this work, and it comes from my experience in the church. The community of the faithful can be an amazing thing. A group of people who pray together can change the world. Yet many churches resemble the empty tomb more than a group of disciples following the risen Christ along "the Way." We all know numerous stories of dead and dying churches, churches busy tearing themselves apart, or churches simply vanishing into irrelevance. This situation is both tragic and unnecessary.

The decline in the organization we call the body of Christ on earth stems from lack of real spiritual leadership. Seminaries turn out graduates who can write academic papers and know the latest theories about church change, but they struggle to form leaders guided by the Holy Spirit. Fortunately, many institutions are trying to remedy this problem by making spiritual formation central to their curriculum. This is vital because individuals guided by the Holy Spirit can understand the movement of God within their own lives and also sense and proclaim that movement within the life of a community. These persons have eyes to see and ears to hear (Matt. 13:16); they walk with Jesus; and, as the waters are calmed, they invite others to walk with Jesus too. It is my hope and prayer that this small volume can be one aid in the creation of such leaders.

I was able to test this book's format with a group of nineteen pastors at a continuing education class at Luther Seminary in St. Paul, Minnesota. During each of twelve sessions together I taught one aspect of spiritual leadership in conjunction with the prayer practices. It was exciting to see the students respond with great enthusiasm to the format. Not only did they find the work spiritually refreshing and deepening, but they recognized the practical application for their ministry. This experience (along with others where I applied these principles in a less structured manner) confirmed the validity and helpfulness of the approach you'll find here. I truly sense that the work will be successful.

Over the past twenty-five years I have seen the practice of prayer spread from the recesses of monastic life into the mainstream of the church. This movement has been exciting to watch and be part of. Now we stand on the edge of this movement's next phase, which the practice of prayer and the manifestations of the Spirit are made known within whole communities. In this work we see the manifestation of the kingdom of God. As we allow Jesus to walk among us, we can indeed see that the kingdom comes near (Luke 10:11), and it is my great desire that more individuals and communities can experience this wonderful life with God.

ONE

LEADING FROM THE SILENCE

TRAVELING COMPANION
Elijah

Be still, and know that I am God!
—*Psalm 46:10*

*M*any years ago, before my baptism, when I wasn't part of an official religion, I decided that the best thing for me to do was combine my desire for a spiritual calling with a job that involved helping people. I decided to become a psychologist. This field focused on change and growth and dealt with people's hearts and minds, so I thought it would be an ideal arena in which to merge my interest in the life of prayer and my desire to be of assistance to others.

After several years spent completing my training, I began to work in secular mental health centers. Quickly I discovered my hope of uniting the spiritual and the secular was not going to be easy. In the secular world the process dominating organizations relies on the efforts, thoughts, and visions of the people in the institution. The Self is God. This is not to say that a lot of good work doesn't go on in such organizations; it does. However, as someone who wanted to bring God into the conversation, I found myself becoming more disappointed and alienated in these settings.

Eventually I found my way into the church. I thought that here at last, God and work in the world could meet. Perhaps you can imagine how I felt when I saw that the church had become as much a secular organization as the mental health center.

Board and committee meetings at the church were exactly like my team meetings in the mental health arena. People talked a lot, argued their points, thought their best thoughts, worried about money, and then voted on what suggestion they considered best. Of course in the church the requisite thirty-second prayer opened the meeting, but even this was dispensed with if no pastor was in the room. After that, as far as I could tell, God had left the building.

What became clear to me was that the culture and process of secularism so dominated people's lives that they had brought them wholeheartedly into the church. The thoroughness of this takeover prevented even the supposed spiritual leaders from reversing the trend; it seemed that in the realm of spiritual leadership, secularization was hard at work. As I mentioned in the introduction, books on spiritual leadership simply take principles of secular leadership dynamics and repackage them for the church with a paragraph about how all the techniques should be done with the guidance of the Holy Spirit. This approach implies that modern spiritual leaders are supposed to look and act like corporate managers and be judged in terms similar to a strategic planner at IBM or Microsoft.

However, at the same time secularism was busy taking over our churches, something else was happening: some people were discovering the spiritual life. Increasingly the laity were abandoning mainline churches for Buddhist retreats or weekends at Benedictine monasteries. They wanted to find God.

Furthermore, as thousands abandoned church politics in favor of prayer retreats, they realized that the process and practice of prayer differed radically from the secular life. They discovered the truth in Paul's words that the Cross is foolishness to the wise of the world (1 Cor. 1:18-19), and people heard in Jesus' call to "follow me" (Mark 2:14) an invitation into a new realm of being.

I wrote *Creating a Life with God* to aid in learning about the life of prayer. The first step of this journey is engaging the prayer practices, taking time to do those things that allow God to create a life with us. Millions of people now embrace these practices to one degree or another. They do them in their living rooms, in their cars, with their friends, on retreat, and sometimes in their churches. This work has been life-changing and faith-stretching, and it has also generated a tremendous desire for *communities* of prayer.

This desire marks the point where the two trends I have observed and described intersect, and it is where this book begins: The church as a secularized organization meets the individuals and small groups who have seen the value of the spiritual life and want their churches to be places of spiritual life. They want their churches to be spiritual organizations, and yet a clear sense of how to accomplish this aim does not exist. There is no living tradition of spiritual leadership that can, again through a series of practices, allow a community to invite God back into the church boardroom. This book is designed to help people who have become pray-ers to become spiritual leaders, people who can guide not only other individuals but whole organizations into the life of prayer.

DWELLING BY THE BROOK

Elijah is one of the great figures of the Bible. A prophet of the Old Testament, he is the one to announce the coming of the Messiah. This great spiritual leader cries, "In the wilderness prepare the way of the LORD" (Isa. 40:3). So powerful was Elijah's testimony that, over a thousand years after his death, the people now called the desert mothers and fathers left their homes in the cities and followed his example, moving into the desert to pursue a life of prayer and silence.

In 1 Kings 17 Elijah receives instruction to dwell by the brook Cherith. Except for a brief sojourn into town to help a widow, Elijah apparently lives in the wilderness for three years. It is worth imagining what this time was like. In the starkly beautiful wilderness east of the Jordan, the hills and wadis echo loneliness and emptiness. The promised drought takes hold of the landscape, and the silence deepens; the vast space becomes overwhelming as the sunbaked rocks and canyons radiate waves of heat and quiet.

This silence is the beginning of spiritual leadership. The Bible tells us that the fear of God is the beginning of wisdom (Prov. 9:10), and I have no doubt that sitting by the brook, Elijah experienced the fear of God. He was alone, without food, knowing his source of water would dry up and he would face the heat and emptiness of the desert. There were no projects, no curriculum, no programs; only Elijah's prayer, faith, and relationship to God sustained him. Elijah was perfectly positioned to listen for God, to allow God to form and create Elijah into the leader that God desired him to be.

A Radical New Vision

Reflecting upon this image of Elijah, we can see how the method of spiritual leadership radically undermines both the vision of secular leadership and the business that pervades our society. Imagine the response of a contemporary church board to Elijah's approach. What would board members think if he told them that for three years he would get nothing done, start nothing new, run no events or activities? Probably they would consider him to be insane, incompetent, or both. He would be fired instantly. Could he be serious? How dare he collect a salary and do nothing in return.

Elijah dares because he is on to something that the secular world doesn't understand. As with personal prayer, silence and listening are the starting points for spiritual leadership. This is true because without listening for God, we are leading only from ourselves, from our own minds and our own ideas. And the only way to listen for God is to be willing to enter into the silence of prayer, the stillness of doing nothing.

When we enter into this silence, we are seeking—and eventually we encounter—something profound: the freedom of God. The silence of prayer separates us from our projects and our need to be in control of every aspect of our lives, and when we allow this to occur, we are free to let God do with us as God desires. Spiritual leadership requires this freedom from ego, from our "fallen selves." The longer Elijah sat in the desert, the more free he became, free to follow God. In the spiritual tradition, wilderness is the place where we leave the world behind and place ourselves at God's disposal. Paul describes such radical freedom in Galatians (5:1), freedom that is our spiritual birthright if only we will claim it.

We may be surprised, however, that when we first enter into this "holy nothing," we initially encounter not God but ourselves—our own fears and uncertainties, our own projects, habits, hopes, and fears. Meeting our "self" in this way is difficult, and we must learn to sit with these obstacles as we become still so that we may know that God is God.

In the context of leading a community into silence, this encounter with ourselves is far more challenging because we also encounter the "self" of the organization. We meet the collective ego of an organization that, like our solitary ego, needs to be fed and satisfied. This ego expresses itself in the anxieties of the members, the complaints, the demands, the seemingly endless barrage of advice about "how to run a church." Organizations—churches—experience a fear of emptiness similar to that of individuals. The group of people who make up a particular church has the same fears that individuals do: nothing will get done; nothing will happen; our leader is being lazy. For people in the modern world where business is the divine, a church entering into the silence of prayer reacts in horror just as we as individuals do.

LET US PRAY

Recently I spent a week teaching on a seminary campus. Every day students and teachers went to chapel; all the classes let out so we could go to worship together. After the initial welcome and announcements, the woman who began the worship services said, "Now let us take time in silence to prepare our hearts for worship." Every day I timed this "time in silence"; it never lasted more than nine seconds. After I pointed this out to my class, one member commented, "Yeah, I didn't even have time to close my eyes before we were on to the next part of the service."

In our corporate expressions of worship, silence seems to be regarded as something to be rigorously avoided. Contrast the three years of Elijah's silence with the nine seconds of silence in chapel. How much listening can be done in nine seconds?

Similarly, anything but silence fills the work life of a modern church leader. I have asked hundreds of pastors, youth workers, and church staff members how much time they allocate during their workday for prayer practices and silence. Well over 90 percent of them say no time at all. Again, how much listening can be done when no time is allocated for God?

A Practiced Approach to Silence

If silence is the foundational practice for both a personal prayer life and the prayer life of a spiritual leader, then it is necessary to integrate silence into the job of ministry. But how do you do this, and what obstacles will you encounter?

The first step is to commit to the personal practices of prayer, practices that take place in the silence of listening. These practices are outlined in *Creating a Life with God*, and several can be found in the appendix of this book as well.

However, as a leader, this step is only the beginning, for the silence must become part of your vocation, not a personal or separate activity that you practice by yourself in your "free time." Many church leaders have attempted to take this approach to prayer. They vow to get up an hour earlier or stay up an hour later, taking more time from their families and becoming even more exhausted in the process.

Also, this personal approach to prayer communicates the message that prayer exists apart from the life of the community and the job of the spiritual leader. Consequently people regard silence as an extra oddity for pastors to engage in but not essential to the work of the church. This message is the antithesis of what the life of prayer entails. Silence is indeed the work of the church. Prayer is not another program to be undertaken by a strange few but is *the* program, the one activity that undergirds all activities. The spiritual leader needs to convey this reality through action. Therefore, it is essential that silence become a regular and normal part of a leader's workweek and also a part of the community's corporate worship experience.

There are many ways to accomplish these goals. As a leader, begin with your own job time: schedule silence into the workday just like any other activity. In this regard, the Day-timer is your friend. Put prayer on your agenda, on the church calendar, in the bulletin. Use the corporate prayer spaces of the church, and let everyone know that at certain designated times of the week you will be praying in the sanctuary or in the prayer chapel of the church, and invite anyone who wishes to join you. Of course, most of the time you will be alone, but that is not the point. Rather, the point is that people will come to expect their spiritual leader to be praying. They will realize that silent prayer is an essential aspect of the job.

Corporate Silence

Elijah didn't stay in the desert forever. Eventually God told him to reengage with the world; God called him into spiritual leadership—encouraging others to turn to God. Obvious as it may sound, the task of the spiritual leader does need to be clearly stated: help others learn to relate to Jesus. The spiritual leader does not relate to Jesus on behalf of everybody else, although unfortunately many people put their pastor in this role.

Therefore, moving into silence needs to be a corporate endeavor. The leader does not spend time in silent prayer so that everyone else can be extra noisy; rather, the leader facilitates everyone's moving into that space of listening to God. This move can happen in several ways in multiple dimensions of the church organization.

The first dimension involves the staff. Once times are established for silent prayer in the church, then the staff can be required to participate in these times of quiet. Church staff should see this requirement as part of their job. They are part of the praying, listening community, and they need to spend time listening as well.

Using the word *require* may distress people. That distress indicates how secular the church has become. We don't think twice about requiring staff to run programs, answer the phones, go to committee meetings, have a cell phone, or fill out time sheets. Yet to many it seems bizarre or inappropriate to require people who run a spiritual organization to pray, to engage in the one activity that encourages their relationship with the One supposedly in charge of the organization: God.

Second, silence can be introduced into worship. There are many places in the order of worship, no matter what a church's worship style, where silence can be added. A specific time for silent prayer could be introduced, although such an addition is the most radical technique.

For a more gentle approach, simply stretch out the periods of silence that already exist in the worship service. For example, every time you say, "Let us pray," a moment of silence follows. Instead of proceeding after that one second, allow silence to continue for five or even ten seconds. Whenever one person sits down and another gets up for an element in the service, the new leader can wait for an extra moment or two before starting that segment of worship. This technique allows people to become more comfortable with silence. (Chapter 7 discusses the importance of teaching worshipers about these changes in conjunction with introducing them.)

As comfort with silence grows, it will be possible to add longer periods of silence to the worship service. Silence also can be incorporated into special or seasonal services, such as Lent and Advent, when themes of waiting are prominent in worship.

Finally, introduce silence into church meetings. Remember that spiritual leadership involves transforming the organization of the church—not adding another program. Thus all the gathering times already in place present opportunities ripe for prayer. Committee meetings are just small groups within the church. Try adding silence to the beginning and end of such meetings. Ask a committee to spend time in silence before making a big decision or when a major issue requires reflection. Through such action, people within the church begin to get the idea that the whole community is listening for God, not just a chosen few. Every member of the church realizes that this listening is their calling and one essential aspect of being a follower of Jesus.

"After many days the word of the LORD came to Elijah" (1 Kings 18:1). This is what the silence is for; we wait for the word of the Lord to us, the word we need to live the spiritual life and to become spiritual leaders. We enter into the quiet of our own wilderness seeking such a word, and it is here, in faith, that we know God will eventually come to us.

TWO

PRAYING THE BIBLE
Entering the World of Scripture

TRAVELING COMPANION
Wisdom

Wisdom has built her house,
she has hewn her seven pillars.
She has slaughtered her animals, she has mixed her wine,
she has also set her table.
She has sent out her servant girls, she calls
from the highest places in the town,
"You that are simple, turn in here!"
To those without sense she says,
"Come, eat of my bread
and drink of the wine I have mixed.
Lay aside immaturity, and live,
and walk in the way of insight."

—*Proverbs 9:1-6*

hese days, the Bible confuses us. Christians, churches, and the general church culture often seem unclear about exactly what the Bible is and how to approach it. Many consider it a document to be taken literally, even though this is not truly possible. Others regard it as a historical document to be picked apart, analyzed, and perhaps ultimately discarded or set on a shelf next to other important books. Christians in different factions use the Bible to attack one another, even if only figuratively. Finally, some find the Bible a book of great value, once they can find passages they like, those texts that reinforce what they already believe about God.

From the perspective of the spiritual life, the Bible is none of these things; rather, it is a living world to be entered, a world from which God speaks to us.

Wisdom, that powerful feminine figure of the book of Proverbs, is one of the great spiritual leaders of the Bible. She is the "master worker" (Prov. 8:30) who, with God, creates the world. The preeminent teacher, she lifts us out of simpleness and calls us to walk in the way of insight.

In Proverbs 9 we hear that Wisdom builds a house into which we are invited. Perhaps we can imagine going to such a place. It would be beautiful—superb architecture with graceful columns; adorned with works of art; colorful, uplifting light coming in everywhere. The food at the feast would be delicious and well prepared; the hospitality, unparalleled.

After being fed, we would be invited into Wisdom's classroom. What sort of curriculum would we find here? As we read the rest of Proverbs, we can begin to fathom the answer to this question. Part of our learning would involve memorizing and understanding the commandments of

God. But more important would be coming to recognize the paths of wisdom in the midst of making choices in our everyday lives. This is the "way of insight." The many sayings in the book of Proverbs show us how the wise and the foolish act when confronted with common choices that we all face every day.

The practice of biblical prayer allows spiritual leaders to live in Wisdom's house as Wisdom also lives in their world, in their own place and time.

SACRED READING:
LETTING GO OF MINISTRY MODELS

LECTIO DIVINA, or sacred reading (see appendix for an outline of the technique), is the practice of praying with the Bible in order to hear God talking to us out of scripture. For individuals, the practice allows us to deepen our relationship with God and engage the divine in a conversation that promotes our spiritual formation.

For spiritual leaders, sacred reading goes a step further. Because leaders are charged with guiding a community, however large or small, they are called to see how God is leading that community into God's reign. Thus for leaders, sacred reading conditions them to see their world in light of the biblical world, to see how God is calling their community in the way that God has called the communities of biblical times.

Current conventional secular ministry practice encourages leaders to understand and try to apply various models of ministry to their church or ministry site. As models come and go, waves of the latest fashion sweep through the churches: suddenly everyone is doing small-group ministry or purpose-driven ministry or even spiritual ministry, and so on. This market-driven approach to ministry resembles a faith formed by the law. In this approach, which Paul refers to as slavery (Gal. 5:1), we are subject to an external set of parameters that is to be forced onto every situation, every town, every community, every church. This approach denies the living reality of a resurrected Christ who frees us to follow a living, immanent God.

Of course, techniques are helpful. It is good to know how to run a small group, how to do prayer practices, how to play games with youth, how to lead Bible studies. The law does have value. However, from the perspective of spiritual leadership, these skills do not drive ministry; what drives ministry is communication with God.

The Bible tells the stories of many types of communities: growing communities and dying communities, exiled communities and communities in transition, rich communities and poor communities. In all situations God enters in; God speaks; God acts; God saves. Sacred reading, the practice of praying with scripture, allows us to enter these communities and then see our community in the same light. In this process Wisdom calls us and guides us, revealing how God would have us lead and act such that our own community can move closer to the kingdom.

ENCOUNTERING FEAR:
THE OBSTACLE TO SPIRITUAL LEADERSHIP

You may say, "This sounds great. I'd love to follow as Jesus helps me lead my church." At this point it is worthwhile to discuss the main obstacle to spiritual leadership—fear.

Church leaders today are highly conditioned to one view of leadership and success: growth and increasing numbers. Following scripture is terrific as long as we are reading the story of Jesus feeding the five thousand or one of the stories where throngs greet him. This is the way our churches "should" look, the way they would look if we were really successful. We don't want to lead the exile communities of the prophets or the enslaved community of Egypt or the starving, dying communities of Kings or the oppressed communities described at the beginning of Matthew where babies are slaughtered (2:16-18). Leading these communities would render us unsuccessful, worthy only of being fired.

A friend told me a story about a youth minister who submitted his monthly calendar to the senior pastor as part of a job review. The calendar came back to him with a large red X marked in every date where no event appeared. He was told that he wasn't working hard enough, that he wasn't getting enough kids to come, that he was fired. Spiritual leaders fear being judged in this one way—as either a success or a failure based solely upon numbers.

If we live in this fear, we can never allow ourselves to listen to God. This is the pivotal choice every spiritual leader must make: serve God or serve our fear. If we serve our fear, we will be enslaved to the ways of the world and the egos of those around us who seek to control our lives. If we serve God, we will fearlessly be able to see and discern how God is working for life and growth in every situation, large and small.

Although this choice may sound easy to make, it is not. The challenge of choosing God makes the personal prayer life of the leader supremely important. If we are to cling to the Rock (1 Cor. 10:4) that is our salvation, then we must practice holding on to Jesus through and in spite of our fears and anxieties.

This issue surfaced in a powerful and painful way at a prayer retreat I led. The participants at this event, all spiritual leaders, engaged in long periods of silent prayer. Inevitably they encountered their fear of failing and being fired from their jobs, perhaps even ending up homeless and in the gutter. They did not experience this feeling as simply a passing concern but rather in a vivid and deeply visceral manner.

When simple reassurance failed to calm them, I made these leaders an offer. I told the participants that I was so sure they would find a path God had prepared for them if they followed God in the life of prayer that should they indeed ever become homeless and jobless as a result of following the spiritual life, they could call me. I promised to fly them to my home and give them a place to live and work to do.

Years later I have yet to receive one phone call.

How to Enter the Biblical World

As a leader, how do you assist your community to enter into Wisdom's house? You'll find a similar pattern of advice in the how-to sections of this book. It is the Nike way: "Just do it."

As with everything a leader does, start with yourself. You must find time to practice sacred reading either individually or regularly with a group.

For pastors, a marvelous opportunity for sacred reading lies in sermon preparation. Unfortunately seminaries train students to approach sermon preparation in the same way as writing an academic essay. Consult the commentaries, find illustrations, craft a well-constructed manuscript, or, if all else fails, download something from the Internet.

A different approach is to pray your sermons. Whatever the scripture for the coming Sunday, use the practice of sacred reading to live with the passage for the week. As you enter into prayer with the scripture, what words and phrases stand out for you? What images come to mind? How is God talking to you about your life, about the life of the community and of the world? These observations are gifts from God to be proclaimed in worship. They are the paths of peace (Prov. 3:17) that Wisdom is revealing to you. They are the truths, the good news, that you as a leader are called to share with others.

If you do not preach in your particular ministry, this approach can work with other leadership opportunities. If you teach or lead groups, run Christian education programs, counsel, or administer a nonchurch ministry, sacred reading can always be a source of inspiration and wisdom guiding what you do or say in ministry.

As mentioned earlier, leaders can use sacred reading in personal prayer life to answer the questions *What kind of community am I in?* and *With what issues in my community is God working?* As you pray into the biblical story, you come to recognize your own community in the life of the Bible. You then come to see how God speaks to and works with such a community. This vision can be an incredibly powerful guide as you seek to do ministry.

For example, I live in a farming community. The Bible talks a lot about farming and issues related to agrarian society, and many problems of our town are problems that Israelite farmers faced—for instance, the loss of smaller family farms and the resulting depopulation of the land (Isa. 5:1-10). The more I pray with the scriptural stories that are also our stories, the more I hear God speaking to us out of the scripture. This experience is invaluable in my ministry because it leads and guides me when I talk to farmers, work with community issues, or simply watch the landscape change in response to human action in a fallen world.

SACRED READING WITH GROUPS

At a recent meeting concerning the budget for a large project, an architect who considers herself a spiritual person said to me, "Well, okay, there's the faith approach over here and the real world over here," gesturing with her hands to show the divide. This incident beautifully illustrates what spiritual leaders are up against.

Even faith-filled people have been thoroughly secularized when it comes to life in the world. There is faith "over here" (presumably useful for personal matters and certain life transitions), and there is the real world "over here," which covers all the important stuff like money, jobs, and everything else. According to this view, biblical stories served folks who lived in a faraway magical time when people met angels of the Lord on the road, but they aren't much use for those of us who live in the modern, scientific world.

If church communities, and even broader communities, are to function as spiritual communities, this vision of reality must be transformed. Sacred reading in groups provides a powerful tool for such transformation.

By *groups* I don't mean new groups established as part of a program (see chapter 6 for discussion of this kind of group). Rather, spiritual leaders need to focus more on the groups that already exist within the church structure, groups that have largely been secularized.

Most churches have one or more groups such as boards, committees, staffs, planning groups, ministry groups, men's groups, women's groups, and so on. In these groups, leaders can introduce the practices of prayer.

Because the Bible is the foundational text of our faith, bringing the practice of sacred reading into the groups of the church is vital. Sacred reading can be adapted for many situations. Options include the long three-step version, a shorter two-step method, or a simple reading. In the latter, a passage of scripture is read twice, followed by a period of silence and an opportunity for people to share what they heard in the reading.

Whatever the specific method, introducing this prayer into the regular life of the church will move the community into the biblical world. As people hear and see God talking to them in the life of scripture and in their own lives, they will begin to realize that the world of faith and the "real world" are not opposite ends of the spectrum but are the one world into which God speaks and acts.

Moving into Wisdom's house through prayer also allows the groups of the church to let go of their own expectations and preconceived notions of what should be happening in their community. This is the movement from the slavery of the law to the freedom of Jesus. As the church lets go of dead ideas and begins to recognize the actual way God is living and moving and working in the church, excitement and energy build. Furthermore, the recognition of spiritual freedom helps create space in the community for the action of the Spirit.

As the groups listen to the observations arising out of *lectio*, they hear this transforming movement of God in the life of the church. In the final phase of the prayer time, participants reflect upon the question *How is God speaking to you?* In individual prayer practice, the answer addresses one person. However, in group practice intended to foster spiritual leadership, the question takes on both individual and collective functions. Thus each person's observations say something about how God speaks to that individual but also give clues as to how God is speaking to the ministry and activity of the group and the church as a whole.

The group leader gathers the observations and reflections and points out common themes and stirrings. For example, the leader might notice that many people in the group talk about care for the poor or concern about an issue in the community at large. These observations might be pointing the church in the direction of a specific mission project or new ministry.

Ideally, all the groups in a church would do some form of biblical prayer. However, especially at first, this kind of saturation may not be possible. Thus leaders need to decide where to introduce the practice. If the church has a staff group, this would be the best place to start. In a smaller setting without other staff, a board or other group of lay leaders would be a good starting point. These guidelines apply similarly to a nonchurch organization.

Once the community begins to pray the Bible, wonderful things start to happen. Whatever size or shape, location or situation, the community that listens to Wisdom's cry is a church that lives:

And now, my children, listen to me:
    happy are those who keep my ways.
Hear instruction and be wise,
    and do not neglect it.
Happy is the one who listens to me,
    watching daily at my gates,

waiting beside my doors.
For whoever finds me finds life
    and obtains favor from the LORD;
but those who miss me injure themselves;
    all who hate me love death.
                            —Proverbs 8:32-36

THREE

NO OTHER GODS
Contemplative Concentration and the Jesus Prayer

TRAVELING COMPANION
Moses

*I am the LORD your God, who brought you out of the
land of Egypt, out of the house of slavery; you shall
have no other gods before me.
You shall not make for yourself an idol, whether
in the form of anything that is in heaven above,
or that is on the earth beneath, or that is in the water
under the earth. You shall not bow down to
them or worship them.*

—Deuteronomy 5:6-9

The image of the spiritual leader emerging from silence, holding the book that contains God's word, is the image of Moses coming down from Mount Sinai. He had stood in the cloud upon the mountain, had met God, and had been given tablets engraved with sacred scriptures. Yet when he returned to the camp where the people were, he was greeted with the people's idolatry of the golden calf.

The previous two chapters dealt with the fundamental elements of both the spiritual life and spiritual leadership—silence and scripture. The following chapters will build upon these fundamentals by each highlighting a specific aspect or issue in spiritual leadership. Ultimately the goal of spiritual life and leadership is to help God form the spiritual communities that are manifestations of the church on earth. Thus each chapter will look at obstacles to the formation of such communities and explore how a certain type of prayer practice can assist in overcoming that obstacle. In this way I hope to show how the spiritual life can flow into spiritual leadership, which in turn can foster spiritual community.

In the Bible, we recognize idolatry as one of the greatest sins committed by humans. Thus it may be no surprise that idolatry is one of the most important issues for spiritual leaders to address.

Idols are whatever bind and enslave us and prevent our seeing, worshiping, and following the true God. Moses is emblematic of the spiritual leader who brings God's people from bondage into freedom, liberating them from the idolatry that holds them captive. As Moses learned, this is an ongoing issue, one that the spiritual leader always struggles with both in private life and in the life of the church.

The power of idols lies in their ability to distract us. To this day, millions of people travel thousands of miles and spend large sums of money to visit the religious statues in Egypt. I remember as a child reading about the reconstruction of a temple that was moved to make way for the Aswan Dam project on the Nile River. The pictures in *National Geographic* magazine stunned and fascinated me. The intricate, complex reconstruction required highly skilled workers. I was amazed by the discussion about the specifications of the temple: how could these ancient people figure out how to construct an edifice so that the rising sun illuminated a statue deep inside on exactly one day of the year?

These statues and this temple structure are beautiful and powerful. They command our attention, our time, our focus. We can easily understand how they became gods. In our time and place this power to distract is no less prevalent. Consider Las Vegas. This modern temple complex rises from the desert, just as in ancient Egypt. The lights of the casinos can be seen from at least one hundred miles away. The immense palaces of wealth draw thousands, welcoming them with stunning shows and promises of fortune. Modern-day priests ply the people with food, drink, sex, and endless displays of magic and power, and then hypnotize them with spinning wheels, shuffling cards, and occasionally a gift of money. Yet as the dazzle turns the worshipers into zombies, these same priests rob the people of their money and often their very lives.

This idolatrous power is no less prevalent in the church. Anyone who has spent much time in a church community knows the many idols that reside there: the candlesticks that cannot be moved, the rules that cannot change, the order of service that cannot be altered, the only musical instruments that can be played, the donor of large sums who can do as he pleases. All these are idols because we serve them. They have power over us, and thus they rob us of our humanity and our ability to see the one true God who lives and moves in our midst.

BEYOND IDOLATRY

When you recognize idolatry's grip on you or on those whom you lead, a common reaction is anger. Moses reacted that way when he saw the people dancing before the golden calf (Exod. 32:19)! Anger arises in response both to the destructive power of idolatry and to its ability to frustrate leadership. However, although anger does contain energy that can overcome idolatry, ultimately it will destroy you and others. For spiritual leaders, understanding idolatry's prevalence and power brings better results than anger. Understanding idolatry can lead to compassion and to the idol's demise.

The story of the golden calf reveals that idolatry arises when people miss God. This may sound surprising. Idolatry does not occur because people are evil or because they want to ignore God; rather, the cause turns out to be the exact opposite.

As human beings, we long for God's presence. We want to serve God, to see God, to be with God. The problem is that our God is unseen. Only Moses got to see the face of our God, while the people had to wait alone at the foot of the mountain. After a while they began to miss God's presence. They wanted, needed, something to show them God was with them. So they built a golden calf that they could see.

Because our senses are so powerful, the things we can see and touch and taste and feel can easily take the place of a God who, at first pass, is not obviously present. Distraction takes over, and soon we become full-fledged idolaters.

The remedy to the problem of an unseen God is a prayer practice that focuses all our attention upon God. Because the Jesus Prayer develops contemplative concentration, it is ideally suited to address the issue of idolatry. The purpose of this practice is to concentrate the mind on the name and power of Jesus. He is to be the sole object of our mind as we are faithful to the command "You shall have no other gods before me" (Exod. 20:3).

The JESUS PRAYER, a simple repetitive prayer practice, repeats the phrase inspired by the blind beggar who called out to Jesus (Mark 10:47): "Jesus, Son of David, have mercy on me!" (See appendix for more detail.) The mind of the pray-er becomes focused on the power and presence of Jesus. As we pray this prayer, two things happen.

First, we become aware of our own idols. The distractions of our mind rear their heads and attempt to divert our attention. Our projects, our habits and patterns of behavior, whatever we are anxious about, all become very clear to us as we strive to focus on Christ.

Second, these idols begin to lose their power over us. The more we focus our mind upon Jesus, the more he comes to live in our heart and mind, occupying the central place that a god inhabits. With each repetition of the prayer, Jesus becomes more real. Jesus becomes more alive and powerful in our life; Jesus becomes the one God on whom we concentrate to the exclusion of all other gods.

Uncovering Your Own Idols

How do leaders begin the process of dismantling idolatry? Start by looking at your own idols as well as the idols in your community. As you pray the Jesus Prayer and discover the distractions that arise in your own mind, God reveals those things that you have given power in your life. Spiritual leaders in modern church communities face three particularly potent idols: being liked, pleasing people, and dependence on the pastor.

People in the helping professions often have a great need to be liked. They crave acceptance from others. That need may derive from their own sense of emptiness, their own wounds. In the church, this reality may cause pastors to spend a great deal of time and energy on issues related to their own approval. Congregations unconsciously sense this kind of neediness and can then use it to control their pastors. The result is often disastrous for everyone: a pastor running scared, afraid to do anything that will distress people, and a congregation becoming increasingly dependent on a pastor who compulsively offers to help everyone.

The flip side of a dependent congregation is a controlling congregation: members know their disapproval could send the pastor into anxious retreat. This idolatrous cycle of need and dependency pulls the focus of the community far from God.

Imagine if Moses had functioned out of need for approval. Probably the people of Israel would have walked right back into Egypt. Or they would be worshiping the golden calf to this very day. Luckily Moses was free of this pattern of behavior. When the people grumbled or needed something, Moses didn't cringe or regard their needs as a personal failure; rather, he did one simple thing: he turned to God. Moses used his deep and intimate relationship with God as the source of living inspiration and truth to handle the situations he faced.

In order to stop bowing at the idol of approval or pathological need to help, the hole in the heart—your internal emptiness—must be filled. Practicing the Jesus Prayer helps fill that hole with God. As you are infused with the power of Christ through the working of the Spirit, you no longer bow at the idol of approval or pathological need to "help." Your relationship with God gives you the strength and the wholeness required to face difficult situations and make challenging decisions without being held captive by a dynamic of dependency. Being liberated from the slavery of idol worship allows you the freedom to follow God.

Overcoming Corporate Idolatry

Although liberation from slavery sounds wonderful, in the process you again encounter that great obstacle to spiritual leadership: fear. Even though idolatry leads to death, it can also offer comfort. Your idols are visible and habit-forming, well known and easy to manage. It has been said that we prefer the prison we know to the freedom that is a mystery.

The Jesus Prayer draws you into new territory, into the silence where you will encounter the divine. You do not know what God will have in store, where God will lead and challenge you.

Many people I have talked to as they enter into the life of prayer have reported that at some point they would rather not hear what God has to say to them. This fear keeps us in bondage. It is the fear that leaders must allow

God to transform if they are to assist others to become free of fear and relate more deeply to God.

Scripture repeatedly tells us, "Do not fear" (for example, Isa. 44:2 and numerous other occurrences), for God is with us. God will see us through fire and flood (Isa. 43:2). This is easy to say but far harder to live. Consider the Jesus Prayer a lifeline while moving through these dangers into the promised land of faith and the presence of God. And once others see us, the leaders, making this journey, then they too are ready and able to make it.

Recently I listened to another in a long line of church horror stories. The congregation, predominantly Caucasian, hired a new pastor, a very learned young man with a non-Caucasian wife, and within a year he was run out of town. Over the course of those twelve months, among other things, his computer was broken into to make sure it contained no pornography; his wife was treated in a horribly racist manner; and he was falsely accused of numerous blunders and scandals.

Why? The primary reasons were his use of a liturgy designed for recently merged denominations rather than the older denomination's liturgy and the fact that his wife wasn't the same race as the majority of the congregation. This young couple was sacrificed upon the altar of that congregation's idols.

Just as idolatry is rampant in the world, so too it is rampant in our congregations. Again, this is not because the people of the church are evil but rather because the church has a long history of, perhaps inadvertently, promoting and creating idols through the secularization process described in previous chapters.

By focusing on rules and regulations, on habits and patterns of behavior, churches have turned "the way we've always done it" into a god. When the young pastor described above began doing things the way the new denomination had trained him, he ran afoul of this idol, who then demanded his blood.

By refocusing a community on Jesus, a spiritual leader can lead people out of such collective imprisonment to idol worship. The process of contemplative concentration, as demonstrated by the Jesus Prayer, can aid the process.

In the first step of the process the spiritual leader comes to understand the power of idolatry through his or her own practice. Only by appreciating idolatry's impact will a leader be able to address the issue with others and help them see how corporate idols bind the community.

I remember a conversation with a church member about the candles on the altar. The individual was angry because the candles had been moved one Sunday to make room for a piece of liturgical art. In this conversation we were able to explore the importance of these objects and how it did seem that when the candles weren't there, God wasn't there. Through this interaction I was able to redirect the person's attention toward Jesus rather than toward the candles.

The second step in the process is to draw people into the practice of focusing on God, who is above all idols. Among many ways to approach this, one is to introduce the Jesus Prayer into worship. It could be included in a corporate confession, sung as a repetitive chant, or simply repeated silently at some point. The Jesus Prayer also can be incorporated into the small groups of the church. Board meetings can begin with five minutes of the Jesus Prayer.

Small-group ministries can adopt it as an opening prayer time. Many opportunities exist. This particular practice communicates to the community that Jesus is the focus. Not the candles, not the style of liturgy, not "the way we've always done it."

In the third step, name the progression toward idolatry and the way of liberation. The Bible is so clear in discussing these two processes, and yet inside the church we often refuse to point them out. This very fact demonstrates both the power of the idols and the power of fear. The silence of leaders, in this case a silence born not out of prayer but out of fear, gives the idols their power. Spiritual leaders need to shine the light of Christ onto this phenomenon so that the idols lose their power.

This naming can occur in many ways: in teaching and preaching, in individual discussions with people, in an intentional conversation with groups in the church. In participating in such conversations in churches, I notice that most people know this move toward idolatry is occurring. They know certain behaviors or habits hold the community prisoner. They know an almost demonic resistance to change exists; and, amazingly enough, the majority of people hate their imprisonment!

This awareness coupled with a seeming inability to change point to the importance of spiritual leadership. Groups of people need leaders. God raised up Moses and the other leaders portrayed in scripture because people need examples to follow, not only to give them courage but also to show them this "new thing," this "way in the wilderness" (Isa. 43:19). Until a leader who knows the way out of idolatry through personal experience can point out the path for others, the community will remain stuck and bound.

Insight into this path of liberation comes from people whose church has been destroyed by flood or fire. They report that the disaster, although painful, was one of the best things to happen to their church. All their idols were destroyed, and all that was left for the congregation was God's call in a new direction. They were freed to begin anew.

Moses understood the importance of eliminating idols when he told the people to destroy the golden calf. Neither modern disaster stories nor the biblical story encourages me to pray for disasters, but they do reveal the liberating effect of removing idols as well as a leader's role in helping to rid a community of idolatry that prevents a focus on God.

"Lord Jesus Christ, Son of God, have mercy on me."

With these simple words, we cry out to God and ask Jesus to come into our darkness and heal us, empower us, transform us. So liberated, we can help others seek God and be liberated. Like Moses, we can help lead people through the wilderness and into the promised land.

FOUR

Silent Contemplative Prayer

Be Still and Know

Traveling Companion
Mary

*Mary treasured all these words and
pondered them in her heart.*
—*Luke 2:19*

he truth is that we are not Moses. We don't go up the mountain to talk to God; we don't receive tablets etched by God's finger; our faces do not glow with the light of God's presence. Although these are perhaps obvious statements, they need to be said aloud because in church culture, there is an expectation that the leaders are God's representatives. Pastors are given tremendous amounts of power over people and their lives. They are also expected to be visionaries, the ones who come up with the latest and greatest ideas for church growth and renewal. And, of course, there is no shortage of people ready to assume and fill this role of Messiah.

Spiritual leadership rejects the notion of leadership by ego and charisma. It challenges the idea that we know what God wants or what God is doing in the life of our particular community. Instead, it begins with the premise that we do not know what God is doing or thinking or creating. Spiritual leadership invites people into the unknown, and one of the most powerful biblical examples of a leader who walked the path of uncertainty is Mary, the mother of Jesus. In fact, she is such a good example of this type of leadership that many may not even regard her as a leader at all! Yet, through the centuries since Easter, Mary has been an inspirational figure to millions who have tried to be Christ's disciples.

So how can you learn from Mary's example, and what sort of prayer practice can help you venture with her into the unknown silence of God? In chapter 1 we looked at silence in general as a key component to spiritual leadership. In this chapter we consider specifically the practice of silent contemplative prayer as a method for entering into silence and for developing leadership qualities that can assist in transforming a community into one that listens for and experiences God's presence.

MARY'S JOURNEY INTO SILENCE

Most Christians are very familiar with Mary's story, yet few have looked at it as a model of leadership. From the moment that the angel came to talk to her (Luke 1:26-27), Mary began a journey into unknown territory. From that point onward her life was not her own; she had no idea what was going to happen to her, to her family, to her people. Although we may give lip service to understanding her position, the vast majority of us would be horrified to adopt such a stance in relation to our own lives.

Recently while teaching at a seminary I had lunch with some students who were beginning to interview for ministerial jobs. One student described a recent phone interview in which the first question was what curriculum he liked to use for confirmation class. Of course he had an answer for this question and was quite happy that his favorite curricula matched those approved by the search committee.

What if this young man had said, "I have no idea what curriculum I would use for confirmation. I need to wait and see what God is going to do with the youth in the community where I am called before I can even begin to consider choosing a curriculum"? My guess is that the interview would have ended right there. Yet this is exactly the radical openness that God called Mary into. Nothing the angel said to her made any sense; nothing about her life after that moment conformed to the patterns of normal life for a young girl in first-century Palestine. Her only response was to ponder in her heart (Luke 2:19) and to wait and see and follow.

Taking the example of the young man and his interview question, perhaps we can make two observations about the church and spiritual leadership. The first is again how much the church has conformed to patterns of the secular world. Just as in a secular business, leaders in the church are expected and required to have answers, to articulate the five-year plan, to adopt and usurp the position of God as the One who creates and reveals the kingdom on earth. The second is the radical nature of spiritual leadership, which runs counter to the first trend. Spiritual leadership is leadership content to ponder, to listen, to wait, to resist the temptation to know, assert, and assuage every human anxiety and desire for certainty.

Approximately thirty-three years elapsed before Mary fully understood the meaning of what the angel first told her. In our fast-food culture, thirty-three years is an impossibly long time to wait. Furthermore, these thirty-three years did not pass peacefully and quietly; rather, those years were marked by turmoil and uncertainty, confusion and revelation, and finally horrendous sadness and death. And through it all Mary waited, watched, and pondered, and ultimately God's will and purpose were revealed. This is the radical waiting of silent contemplation.

LEADERSHIP QUALITIES

The practice of SILENT CONTEMPLATION is both simple and difficult (see appendix for a method of silent contemplation). Sitting for even twenty minutes—drawing attention back to a sacred word, cutting through mental discourse, practicing disinterest in place of our constant proclivity to dwell on ideas, projects, worries, conflicts, or our to-do list—is challenging to say the least. Yet what this practice does, in addition to developing our own relationship with a God who desires to seek us out, is to cultivate three useful and important leadership qualities: humility, clarity, and courage.

Humility is an essential quality for a spiritual leader. Without humility we are always in danger of replacing God with ourselves. Fortunately there is perhaps no better practice for developing humility than silent contemplation. As we enter into the "nothingness" of this practice, we soon realize how little we know about either ourselves or God. Our thoughts and feelings race, often swinging wildly between topics and feeling states. One minute we are anxious about our latest project; the next, we are thinking about an incident in childhood or wondering if we left the coffeepot on at home; any vision of ourselves as brilliant spiritual practitioner quickly dissolves.

Furthermore, God seems to be nowhere in sight. We wonder where are the brilliant insights, the flash of vision for our church, the voice from on high? The God we expected doesn't show up. These experiences develop a humility that derives from a deep-seated understanding that before God we are a tiny creature whose frailties and limited abilities are all too obvious. This type of humility raises in us a desire to be led by God, to hear from God, to wait all the more until God comes to us. We are less in a hurry to get things done, to fix things, to trot out the latest, greatest spiritual gimmick. Rather, we yearn all the more for God's presence and word to us.

The paradox of silent contemplation is that not knowing, this humility born of emptiness, is itself a sign of God's presence with us. As we more fully experience the peace of silent prayer, as the desire for God wells up in us, as we more clearly know that we do not know, we slowly begin to realize that God does not leave or forsake us. In this way, the development of humility leads to the second quality of spiritual leadership, clarity.

The church as an institution generally lacks clarity. As I once heard the predicament described, church is like trying to herd a hundred cats up a hill. People are in a church for a myriad of reasons, many of which run counter to each other. The net result is an absence of direction and focus, a sense of diffuse energy and uncertain aim. Quite simply, the reason is that an organization supposedly focused on God too often actually focuses on the individual concerns of each member.

Spiritual leaders easily become sucked into the cat-herding activity. But chasing each cat hither and yon stirs up more confusion, and soon the leader may be as unclear as anyone else in the organization. I recently heard a story about a head pastor whose enthusiasm for a particular program or direction shifted every few months. Trying to follow the pastor's lead, the staff and the church were always shifting direction, first charging off toward one program, then dropping that one and pursuing another. Naturally, lack of focus, frustration, and confusion reigned.

If we look at Mary's journey through the Gospels, we see a telling pattern. On the one hand, she becomes almost invisible, disappearing from the stories of Jesus in her silence and her humility. Yet, on the other hand, she is obviously still present and focused on her son, such that when he is crucified there she is standing by the cross (John 19:25). Her place in life is clear: she is totally devoted to the path God has laid out for her, and nothing, not even Jesus' apparent disowning of her (Mark 3:31-35), can sway her course.

Silent prayer will help you to focus clearly on God. The constant stream of thoughts that run through your mind is like the hundred cats. At first you go chasing after them, lost in the intrigue of where they go and whether we can catch them. But the more you practice silent contemplation, the less tempted you will be by their antics. Eventually you will barely notice them at all, and when you are distracted by them, you can return more quickly to the open space of the silence where you wait for God.

The clarity you develop in your practice will enhance your leadership. Whatever your position in the church, you will be able to wait for God to reveal God's self in the midst of ministry and stay focused on this revelation as it occurs.

This ability to maintain focus on God's leadership requires not only humility and clarity but also another quality developed in silent contemplative prayer: courage. As described earlier, many spiritual leaders live and work in fear. They are afraid of getting fired; they are afraid of their senior pastors; they are afraid of their boards, the largest donor in the church, or their ecclesial superiors.

The Jesus Prayer counters that fear through the encounter with the power of Jesus. Silent contemplative prayer helps to overcome fear and develop courage because you watch your fears dissolve before God.

As you sit in the silence with nothing to do and nothing to hang on to save the solitary word that grounds you to the present moment, you do indeed face all that you fear. Sometimes you will be tempted to get up from prayer, run out of the sanctuary, and fix whatever problem plagues you during your practice.

Don't succumb to this temptation. Rather, as you continue to sit with your prayer, notice that eventually these fears dissolve, giving way to the reality of grace. Observing this phenomenon in your own mind engenders courageous knowing that God will also work wonders in the life of your community.

Let us again consider the example of Mary. I cannot imagine what it must be like to be a refugee, especially one during the first century. Amazing courage and faith enabled Mary to follow in her calling, even in light of the countercultural nature of that calling. Perhaps she had dreamed of a normal life in her village, looking forward to having a family and, if they were lucky, a livelihood that supported them and kept them relatively safe and well fed. Now, however, God thrust Mary and Joseph into danger and uncertainty with no clear path or model to follow.

Unfortunately this countercultural path of the church is not well understood in our society. It's one thing to say that we are not of the world (John 15:19) while we are able to shop at the mall and live just like anyone else; it is quite another to say that and then try going against the conventions of the day.

Let us look again at the situation of the young man interviewing for the pastoral job. The notion of a canned confirmation curriculum that fits every church in the denomination and the assumption that the best one is the one most successfully marketed are fundamentally secular ideas. They have nothing to do with God. They are part of a model based on current understanding of public education supplemented by market capitalism. However, these assumptions prevail in our churches and seminaries. So, it would have taken remarkable courage for that student to challenge the idea of canned curriculum in an interview and insist that a more appropriate path would be to follow God in a manner unique to time and place—a fundamentally biblical and spiritual notion.

As God comes to us in the silence of our prayer, we are infused with the courage we need to lead toward God. As we sit with the storms of our own mind and watch them settle, we are enveloped with a stillness that can overcome any fear. The stillness of God is a vast space of love and grace that can settle any disturbance within a person or a community. When a leader becomes comfortable inhabiting such a space, then it is possible to enter into leadership in a way that is humble, clear, and full of courage.

INDIVIDUAL PRACTICE

One of the main practical differences between Mary's experience and ours is that Mary didn't really seem to have much of a choice in how her life turned out. This is not to say that she had no choice or did not willingly embark on the path God put before her. At the same time we must acknowledge that the power of God's calling was such that it would have been pretty hard to turn down.

Individuals in church leadership positions have much greater say over how time is spent and how ministry unfolds. They can avoid the practice of prayer; and since "doing nothing" is frowned upon in our culture, it's easy to schedule appointments and all manner of relevant activities in times allotted for silent contemplation.

It is easy to say, "Just practice silent prayer." It is harder to do it. At this point the issue of discipline as an aspect of spiritual leadership comes to the fore. If you are going to be a spiritual leader, then spiritual practice is not optional.

I have spoken to church leaders who say that they sometimes practice or the staff occasionally prays together, but practically speaking, prayer is treated like the person who is "last hired, first fired." Maybe it happens; maybe it doesn't.

Fitting silent contemplation into a schedule is particularly challenging because it seemingly yields no results. Even worse, the experience is sometimes negative rather than positive. Although I have almost never heard anyone describe an experience with *lectio divina* as negative, that is definitely not the case with silent prayer. The experience can be boring, irritating, or confusing. Restlessness, dissatisfaction, and the desire to run away are common. With all of these possible results, why bother?

The answer to this question lies in the answer to a more important question: Do we really believe that God is present and active and will lead us out of the silence? I would maintain that the honest answer for most Christians and for most leaders is no. This is why we are so obsessed with doing and activity. We give God lip service, but we really don't think that if we are quiet long enough, God will show up. Silent prayer places us squarely in the path of the question *Will God appear?* and forces us to engage it in a new, and perhaps very different, way.

Silent contemplation challenges you to put something countercultural and even scary on your schedule. This brave act requires engaging the discipline necessary to stick with the practice. Three means of support in this endeavor are encouragement from others, regular retreats, and spiritual direction.

Connecting with people who are also trying to incorporate silent prayer and other practices into their life and ministry reinforces your own practice. Seek out opportunities to join or form groups where accountability and mutual encouragement can undergird you on your way.

Just as helpful is the practice of attending retreats. Whether organized retreat events or a weekend alone at a retreat center, concentrated time devoted to practice reinforces regular, everyday prayer practice. Retreat experiences can deepen that practice, further encouraging daily prayer. An organized event offers the advantage of providing an opportunity to receive direction or ask questions of someone with more experience or knowledge of the practice.

Finally, spiritual direction, the practice of listening for God with a spiritual friend, nurtures your practice in several ways, not least of which is simple encouragement to continue praying. Unfortunately many people are unfamiliar with the practice of spiritual direction, what happens in a direction session, or how to find a good director. It is beyond the scope of this book to describe these issues in any detail. However, there are many excellent books on spiritual direction (one example is *Holy Listening: The Art of Spiritual Direction* by Margaret Guenther). I recommend exploring this subject and finding a good spiritual director to assist you on your spiritual journey.

CORPORATE PRACTICE AND COMMUNITY TRANSFORMATION

The corporate practice of silent contemplation begins with the prayer of the individual leader. It is important for members of the community to know the leader is engaging in silent contemplation for two reasons.

First, the regular practice of silent prayer makes a statement about a life lived with Christ. It is a radical act by a person sincerely trying to live according to the will of God and not be governed by the rhythms of the world. This concrete action provides leadership for the community and gives the community courage to follow God.

Second, the silent prayer of the leader actually affects the community spiritually. Perhaps you have been to a place where people have prayed for many years such that you can feel the spiritual power there. This feeling is real, not just a hokey idea. When God's presence is invited by the act of someone praying, God shows up. Thus the prayer of the leader acts to invite God into the midst of the community, and this invitation produces results even if the results are not completely clear.

In the next step of corporate silent prayer, others begin participating. As a leader, you can put times of silent prayer on the church calendar and invite members of the congregation, and even the wider community, to join you in this prayer. During these times of contemplation, the church office should be closed and the staff required to participate in the prayer. Even though you and the staff (if the church has any) may be the only ones praying much of the time, this public practice of silence creates a space in your corporate life where God and people regularly listen for God.

As with any of the prayer practices, special programs or retreats appropriate to a church community in its particular place and time can be valuable. In one church where I worked, a small prayer group spent half an hour a week in silent prayer after sharing the needs for healing the community. This prayer group had been in existence for twenty-six years, and the pastor felt certain that this group lay at the heart of the spiritual growth of the church. Specialized prayer groups or ministries like this allow a church to "claim" the corporate practice in a unique way.

As recommended in chapter 1, it is vital to incorporate silent prayer in worship on a regular basis. People will become increasingly comfortable with silence. Then they will begin to connect with their desire for God and subsequently be more interested in seeking God in their lives.

From a leadership point of view, it is relevant to ask, *What are the results of this corporate silent prayer? Are there changes to look for and point to as a fruit of this activity?* A scene in the movie *The Passion of the Christ* depicts Mary, Jesus' mother, and Mary Magdalene wiping up the blood left on the floor after Jesus was scourged. They perform this task in silence while they weep. Unfortunately our communal life often includes conflict and power and the spilling of blood either literally or metaphorically. The church supposedly embodies the opposite process, the process of healing, of reconciliation, of cleaning up the blood. Silent prayer engages this process for the individual and the community. As we become quiet like a child in its mother's arms (Ps. 131:2), we become more able to love God, love ourselves, and love our neighbors (Matt. 22:36-39).

When you begin to see transformation—change—in your community, you are witnessing the fruit of corporate silence. People relax, slow down, soften. Silent prayer allows people to take on the mind of Christ (Phil. 2:5), becoming slow to anger, abounding in mercy, living steadfast in love (Ps. 103:8).

As you witness this unfolding of God's grace in your midst, you will indeed become like Mary, who, as she pondered God's word in her heart, saw the fruit of that word—her baby Jesus—born into the world.

FIVE

EXAMINING SPIRITS
Doing the Will of God

TRAVELING COMPANION
Jesus

[And Jesus said,] "I have come down from heaven, not
to do my own will, but the will of him who sent me."

—John 6:38

I am not a spiritual leader. Perhaps this is the wrong thing to admit. (I'm not sure my publisher would approve!) However, it's an important thing to say. Most books on spiritual leadership I have read devote a lot of space to describing the author's numerous tales of success. This impresses the readers and validates the authority of the author; in our star-studded society we thrive on celebrities whose fame and fortune we regard with wonder. So why don't I make the same claims?

Spiritual leadership from the perspective of the life of prayer is about only one person: God. This is the One who is the focus of all the success and all the activity. To understand my comment "I am not a spiritual leader," just look at the subject of the sentence—I. Spiritual leadership is not about me, my achievements, my success, my vision, or my projects. Rather, it is about what God is doing in the life of the community I serve.

Perhaps this assertion of nonleadership sounds ridiculous or like an attempt at false humility. Or maybe the assertion seems like the splitting of some particularly annoying philosophical hair. But this is not the case; rather, the claim that all spiritual leadership flows only from God is a claim of utmost significance. This claim points to the paradoxical nature of the life of prayer. Yes, leaders obviously "do" things, including leadership, yet at the same time, individuals do not do them, but rather the action flows from God's working in these individuals. Perhaps we can see this more clearly if we look at Jesus himself.

Much has been made of Jesus' "missing years"—the years from his thirteenth birthday to the time he began his ministry at approximately age thirty. Why don't we hear about them? Why don't we come to know of his incredible carpentry skill? Of the beauty of his work, the perfection of his joinery, of how he helped others who needed houses built but couldn't afford them?

Perhaps we can imagine how such information would be sought out in today's world. Surely investigative reporters would be interviewing everyone in Nazareth, trying to ferret out details of Jesus' life: the people he knew, the places he went. I can just see the headlines: "Sixteen-year-old Jesus helps a lame boy," or "Experts marvel at Jesus' cabinetry: 'You can't even see where the pieces of wood come together.'"

In our day we would do everything we could to elevate Jesus to the status of a superstar; in fact, many today try to do this two thousand years after his death on earth. It would all be about him, about his life and achievements, about him as another celebrity. Yet the Gospel record shows that Jesus acted counter to this impulse. Jesus told everyone not to say anything about him. He encouraged those he healed to go give praise to God. He even proclaimed that he was not good but rather that God alone is good (Mark 10:18). In short, he encouraged others to focus only on God, and in this renunciation, "taking the form of a slave" (Phil. 2:7), he was elevated to become revealed as God, as the greatest of all spiritual leaders.

The example of Jesus points to two problems with the current leader-as-superstar model of spiritual leadership. First, it is simply incorrect theologically. The witness of scripture testifies that the Cross is the paradigm of our faith; and, in the Cross the foolish are seen to be wise, while the wise are seen as foolish (1 Cor. 1:18-25). In the vernacular, the superstar is brought low. Jesus focuses not on himself but on the will of the One who sent him (John 6:38).

The second problem is a practical one and follows directly from the first. Only a very few can be superstars in the mold of our secular society. I have seen numerous pastors or youth leaders return from conferences or events wowed by the impressive speakers and tales of church growth, only to rapidly become despondent and depressed when they realize that they can never measure up to the superpastors of our day. Struggling to put into practice the "seven steps" or whatever else should enliven their ministry and bring thousands to their church, they focus more and more on the successful person who has become their hero and less and less on the person who is their Creator and the source of their life and faith.

If we look at this model of hero worship, we can see that it is really an ancient Greek—and thus pagan—model of faith rather than the Christian model of the Cross. In ancient Greece people strove to imitate the hero, who become as strong or as beautiful or as valiant. Those who were endowed with certain skills and abilities were lifted up, while everyone else was left to be envious and empty. The church culture in America today increasingly takes after this model and looks less and less like the community started by the carpenter from Nazareth.

The practice of discernment shows us another way.

Watching from the Still Point

Previous chapters have focused on the spiritual leader as the still point, the one who does nothing but pray. I noted the countercultural nature of this approach, how it is obviously at odds with what our secular society and the secular model of church teach and expect. This stance of stillness is the practice of watching the world from the eye of a storm. In the eye are immense calm and clarity, while all around a tremendous power swirls and moves. And although the focus of everyone's attention is the activity of the storm, meteorology tells us that without the eye—this powerful focal point that holds the swirling winds—the storm would dissipate and cease to exist.

In the practice of spiritual leadership, the storm represents the movement of God in the world of the leader, and the eye is the clear mind of the one who prays. To more fully understand this analogy, we can again look at the life of Jesus. In the story of his temptation in the desert, we see Jesus undergo a kind of death (Luke 4:2). In scripture the number forty is symbolic of a whole lifetime. Forty years in the wilderness produced a new generation of God's people; similarly, after forty days in the desert Jesus would have been dead. But rather than a literal death, what occurs, according to spiritual tradition, is the death of the ego. Satan presents temptations to substitute a human person for God (see Matt. 4:1-11; Luke 4:1-13). In this first death and resurrection, Jesus resists the desire to substitute his will for the will that sent him. When the trial is over, he emerges from the wilderness with the ability to focus on nothing but the God who is revealed in him.

In our prayer practice, in our doing nothing, we also enter into the wilderness and meet the temptations to be great. As we emerge from this experience again and again, we become increasingly clear about our desire to focus on only that which God is doing in our world. Discernment is the practice of this spiritual sight, recognizing the kingdom in our midst.

LED BY THE SPIRIT

The prayer practice known as THE EXAMEN helps us to see the will of God in action (see appendix for the examen technique). The key to understanding the examen as a practice of discernment is to see how looking backward to identify the movement of God can lead to being guided by God into the future.

To see and understand the work of spirits (either the Spirit of God or the spirits of evil) requires observation over time. The Bible illustrates this claim with the example of the fruit tree (see Matt. 12:33 and Gal. 5:22-23). Just as a tree requires an entire season to bear fruit, so too an action in the world requires time to ripen and reveal the nature of the spirit that caused the action.

The examen asks us to look back over a period of time or review an event, looking for glimmers, moments, and actions that appear to be either "of God" or not "of God." The former are the life-giving things that bring the fruits of the Spirit, while the latter are those things that are death-dealing and bring the fruits of a spirit that is not God. This determination may be clear and simple enough. But how does it assist leaders in discerning God's will into the future?

Over time practice of the examen begins to reveal clear patterns in God's action. This should come as no surprise. If we truly believe that God is present and active in our immediate circumstances, then we should also believe that God is at work for good and salvation in these same circumstances. That is, God's action moves in a direction; it works toward something.

We see this truth when we examine Jesus' life. As he traveled about and conducted his ministry, he began to run into trouble with the authorities of his day. He challenged them; he angered them; he did things they considered blasphemous and even evil. This pattern of action eventually led to the cross, a journey and direction that Jesus tried to explain to his disciples (for example, Mark 9:31).

If people who were with Jesus in the middle of his ministry had practiced the examen, they might have discerned two things. The first discernment would have illuminated the past; namely, that the work of Jesus—the healing, the blessings, the confrontations—were "of God." As Jesus himself said, on this day the scriptures were fulfilled (Luke 4:21). The second discernment would have concerned the future; namely, that the pattern of Jesus' actions would lead to a confrontation with the authorities that probably would result in his death. Jesus himself made this discernment, but his disciples had a hard time understanding it.

The prayerful *examen*-ation of the past helps us in our discernment of the future because we begin to see the trajectory of God's action in our place and our time. Once a leader comes to understand and recognize this trajectory, the job of leader is simply to participate in and follow God's lead.

From the Law to the Spirit

As described above, following God's will sounds easy. However, we have already seen that spiritual leadership can put us at odds with the prevailing culture of the church, and this is no less the case with the practice of discernment.

Paul describes the fruits of the Spirit in the letter to the Galatians (Gal. 5:22). In this same work he explores the central metaphor of freedom in the spirit and slavery to the law. Paul describes one of our basic human predicaments: we like to follow rules blindly. We actually enjoy being slaves to the law. It seems easier, less complex, and in our modern world, it sells.

What do I mean? "The law" does not refer just to the set of rules found in Leviticus. The law is any set of religious rules elevated to the status of an idol and then worshiped. Usually we think of these as ecclesial rules, but they can also be curriculum blindly followed or any formula for success in ministry. Without our proclivity to follow such formulas, the ministry publishing business might completely collapse. This is not to say that curricula or rules aren't helpful or even necessary, but it is to say that in a community led by the Spirit of God, we need to hold such directives lightly because our fundamental guide is the Spirit's leadership discerned through prayer.

We substitute the slavery of the law for the freedom of the Spirit because we don't practice discernment and do not know the feeling of security that comes from such a prayer practice. We love the law because we feel that it brings security, but, as Paul tells us, it is the security of death. The security of life comes from doing the will of God, which is true and sure and eternal. Yet if we have not lived and practiced such security, then the freedom of discernment feels like the fear of open space, emptiness, and insecurity.

Recently I had the opportunity to practice discernment with a small group of people interested in ministry. We heard two accounts that helped us understand the difference between following the law and following the Spirit in action. During our time together we reflected upon many aspects of the practice of church. At one point our discussion turned to the practice of preaching. One person related his experience in a poor Central American community. He had noticed that the local people didn't want to listen to preachers who only talked and didn't work with the people. This person had spent time doing physical work with the people and from that position was able to talk to them about Jesus in a very effective way.

Another member of the group, from a North American city, responded that in his church the tradition called for long sermons meticulously prepared by the pastor. He reported that the congregation enjoyed these sermons and that they had resulted in a community well educated theologically and biblically literate.

At this point in the group process two paths were possible. The first would be to take these two experiences and try to extract from them some conclusion about what was "correct" regarding preaching. Unfortunately this is the path most frequently employed in the life of the church, and it is the one governed by the law. If one comes from a tradition that requires preaching, the only choice would be to judge the first example as problematic; then the group might have tried to find a way to make preaching acceptable or successful in the Central American situation.

However, there is another option based on discernment: to see in both stories the search for God's will and the discovery of actions that follow God's will into the future of a particular ministry. In the first example, life-giving ministry was found in working with the people and speaking the good news to them out of that relational position in society. In the second example, life-giving ministry was found through hour-long sermons. In both cases, examining the past gives these two communities clear paths for the future, even if one might mean giving up sermons altogether! The gift of the free woman (Gal. 4:31) is the gift of discernment that sees Christ working in the Spirit through both stories. This gift allows us to lead out of relationship to the Spirit rather than out of "what always has been" or "what should be."

THE DISCERNING LEADER

If you as a spiritual leader wish to engage in the practice of discernment, begin by doing the practice in your own life. This means being willing to look for God's leading from a perspective of nonattachment to outcome, or indifference. That is, you do not expect or prefer any particular result of the discernment prayer. Church leaders find this is a difficult stance because so much in the church is prescribed. For example, what if the discernment led to dropping programs or eliminating parts of the worship service? What if discernment prayer led to starting a new ministry that had no funding? To continue the prayer in the face of such leadings requires courage and freedom from the fear described in previous chapters.

As this freedom becomes more of a reality in your own life, taking time to engage in regular examination of yourself and your ministry becomes easier. Then, from the position of practiced indifference, ask God: *Where is the sense of life, of the leading of the Spirit? Where is the sense of death and an absence of God?* As you address these questions in prayer, you will begin to identify these spiritual movements and can then respond to them.

One trap in the work of discernment relates to this issue of expectations and attachments. I have spoken to many people who practice this prayer, identify that which is of God and not of God, but then become stuck in their discernment. Someone will say to me, "Well, it is clear that this particular program isn't life-giving for me or the church, so I just need to work harder to make it better." If we look at this sentence, we can spot immediately where the problem lies: the focus on the "I" of the leader. A person making a comment like this still holds on to the correctness of a church program and feels the solution is to do something better or different to make it work. Expectation is blocking God's message that the program itself is not of God. Rather than looking for what is of God and moving toward that, some leaders stubbornly hold on to the idea that it is their will, or their church's will, that must prevail and "fix" the program in question. These people are still enslaved; they haven't let go into the realm of freedom.

CORPORATE DISCERNMENT

In the five years of serving my current church, we have been associated with approximately thirty new programs and activities, and not a single one of them was pre-planned or anticipated by the community or myself. Every one of them arose out of the discernment of a group or an individual in the community.

One of the most valuable things you can do as a spiritual leader is to teach and practice the examen with every group in the church and with every individual in the church. The examen can be incorporated into worship, practiced in committee and board meetings, and used with task forces. In all these situations, members of the community learn to ponder this simple question: *Where do you see God working and not working?* As people become used to looking for these spiritual movements and making the commitment to follow them, life in ministry becomes both more simple and more profound. It becomes simple because there is so little worrying and fretting to do. Wherever God leads, that's where you go, period. Life becomes more profound because now you are doing ministry not out of your will and preferences but out of the will and preferences of God.

In groups, the challenge of the examen is listening for the voice of God amid the voices of all the members of the group. This is where the leader's individual practice and familiarity with discernment can prove beneficial. One pitfall of a group examen is the temptation for some people to twist the practice into a means of arguing for or voting for what is "correct." To avoid this, structure the group sessions in a way that allows all the members to speak their observations in a safe environment. Instruct members of the group that listening is as much a part of the practice as speaking, and point out that prayer is listening for the will of God, not lobbying for one's own position.

After people have shared their observations, give everyone time to reflect upon the question: *What are the common themes that we are hearing?* These themes may reveal the workings of God in the life of the group.

For example, the church board may practice the examen together, reflecting on where each person has seen God in the life of the church since the board met last. This is an open-ended sort of examen. Yet, in the sharing time, every member mentions one particular event or activity that happened during the previous month. It would be enlightening to observe this common reflection. After that observation, the board might conclude that they should figure out how to continue or support particular activities that seem to be very much of God.

Finally, it is essential that discernment be consistent and ongoing. It cannot be done once or twice and then stopped. Using the above example, the board would continue to perform the examen on the particular activity everyone noticed as being of God. Their aim is to observe whether God continues to be present in that work over time. Lack of continuing discernment poses a big problem in churches. Almost every church I've been a part of maintains activities that long ago ceased to be life-giving but are still done because once they got started, they could not be stopped. One of the roles of a leader is to encourage ongoing discernment so that the work of the Spirit can continue to move through the community of faith.

WHAT IS SUCCESS?

What is success? I end the chapter with this critical question; critical because leaders are so often judged by whether they are "successful" or not. Furthermore, in our culture being successful is not only highly valued but it is also defined in particular and narrow ways. In the church success means big numbers, lots of programs, lots of activity— a kind of Jesus Wal-Mart.

Interestingly, even Jesus didn't live up to this myopic view of success. By the end of his life all he had was a few followers who were afraid and huddled in an upper room. There was no earthly kingdom; the Romans were still in power; and most of the five thousand were nowhere to be seen.

From the perspective of spiritual leadership success is myriad and multifaceted. Success can be a megachurch, but it can also be a house church. It can be a highly pro-grammatic community, but it can also be a few people who live together based on a rule of life that seeks to do nothing other than follow God.

From the point of view of those who practice the examination of spirits, success means exactly one thing, and it is what Jesus pointed to: following the will of God in your place and your time, no matter where it leads.

SIX

TO CREATE IS TO PRAY
Creativity and the Divine

TRAVELING COMPANION
Solomon

I intend to build a house for the name of the LORD my God, as the LORD said to my father David, "Your son, whom I will set on your throne in your place, shall build the house for my name."

—*1 Kings 5:5*

A Song of Ascents. Of Solomon.
Unless the LORD builds the house,
those who build it labor in vain.
Unless the LORD guards the city,
the guard keeps watch in vain.
It is in vain that you rise up early
and go late to rest,
eating the bread of anxious toil;
for he gives sleep to his beloved.
—*Psalm 127:1-2*

*T*he discussion of discernment and the examen prayer leads directly into the topic of this chapter, creative prayer and the issue of work. As we are guided by the will of God, we move into the realm of action and creation: *What does the church, or any other organization, that wishes to be Spirit-led do? And not only what does the church do, but how does it do it?* Connected to these questions is another one: *In an organization defined by spiritual leadership, who works?*

TOXIC WORK

In the world of the church, something has gone awry with the way we relate to work. It's not just that people who work in the church are overworked and underpaid; the problem goes much deeper than that. Consider any type of church work issue: recruiting volunteers for funerals or Sunday school, the number of hours that a pastor works, the demands on church staff, the fact that youth workers remain in their jobs an average of eighteen months; and, a common theme appears. The nature of work in the church seems, for many people, to have changed from life-giving service to Jesus into exhausting, anger-producing drudgery.

This problem came into clear focus when I began to hear pastors say, "I wish I could go somewhere and worship occasionally because on Sundays all I do is work." If we look at this statement, we begin to understand the nature and depth of the difficulty. Worship is the central activity of the community of faith. Without worship a church is merely another club or social service agency. Furthermore, for the church as an organization to move beyond either of these secular designations, God as revealed in worship must move and live in the heart of the community.

Basic organizational psychology informs us that the nature of a group or an organization usually reflects the nature of the leader. Thus, in a church setting, if the spiritual leader is not worshiping during worship, neither is the congregation.

I once experienced this phenomenon vividly at a church I visited in another community. My family and I sat in the pew and began to struggle with the ten-page bulletin whose inserts were always jumping onto the floor. After a while, amid the noise of those sitting around us, I realized something was happening at the front of the sanctuary. As the worship leaders gave the announcements and then began "working through" the order of service, I looked at the people around me to see what they were doing in response to the activity up front. The children in the row ahead of us were playing on their Gameboys, while their parents chatted. The people behind us were balancing their checkbook. To our right a couple mulled over their date books. None of this activity ceased or changed throughout the "worship service." By the time we were done, I was wondering what any of us were doing there.

For a church community, the implications of this disconnected reality are profound. If no one is really worshiping, then we must ask if God is really present in the life of that organization. If the leader doesn't worship but replaces this most vital activity with "work," then work will be resented and seen as an obstacle to God.

In addition, if the people aren't being fed by Jesus in worship, then they will become all the more needy and demand to be fed by the pastor or the church staff. This will require even more work by this staff as they try to fill needs that should be filled by God.

Now add to these issues the fact that our society's model of work is both compulsive and hyperactive, driven by a need for ever-increasing efficiency and productivity. Taken together, these trends create a work environment that is toxic. People who should be spiritual leaders become burned-out drones whose own spiritual needs go unmet and who wonder what happened to that life-giving call Jesus spoke to them before they attended seminary or began working in the church.

From the perspective of spiritual leadership, the remedy for this sad situation requires that we ask the question *Who works?*

SOLOMON BUILDS A TEMPLE

The rulers of the young Israelite kingdom desired to build a temple. Where was God going to live? The people had the ark in their midst, but their leader, David, felt that God needed a house, a proper place for the "glory" of God.

David wanted to build this temple. As one of the first great kings, he no doubt felt it was a proper thing for him to do—a project fit for a king.

Let us imagine David as a pastor in a modern church setting. What would have happened next? Of course he would have formed a committee. The committee members would meet and plan, hire an architect, start a capital campaign. Then there would be arguments over the size and placement of the kitchen. Of course the "best families" would have the most say over the design.

At some point, though, things would begin to go wrong. The money wouldn't come in on schedule. Or perhaps the builders would embezzle funds. Maybe the denominational loan wouldn't come through. Or the church might split. Whatever the exact circumstances, as time went on, it would begin to seem less and less likely that the building would get built.

At first David's response would just be to try harder. He would create a new committee, hire a more expensive consultant, spend more time at work. He would think, *The Temple must get built. It is the crowning achievement of my ministry.*

Eventually however, it would become clear that the Temple wasn't going to get built. Maybe the church would fire David. Or he might be moved to another parish. The board would decide that he was incompetent after all, not the great leader he was cracked up to be.

Then along comes the next pastor, Solomon. And miraculously, with little effort and with much rejoicing, the Temple gets built in short order. The people proclaim Solomon as a great and brilliant leader. But Solomon knows that something else is at work.

Who Works?

Work is ultimately about creation. We apply ourselves to a particular situation in the world and our energy, our work, changes that situation and creates something new. Whether this is a physical creation, as in the case of construction, or an organizational creation, as in the case of management, or the creation of a more healthy, happy person, as in the case of the helping professions, work is about creation and creativity.

Our normal conception of work is that we *do* it. We apply our body and our mind in some fashion, and the result is that the work gets done. So work is up to us, and the more we work and the harder we try, the greater the result. This understanding of work fits perfectly with our self-centered view of reality. Just like the "I" at the center of our discussion of discernment, viewing ourselves as the central locus of work is the behavior of a creature who has mistaken itself for the Creator.

Solomon understood work differently. He knew that David couldn't build the Temple, because God didn't want him to. Similarly, Solomon was able to complete the project because God ordained it. Neither act had anything to do with how hard each man worked. In the psalm attributed to him, Solomon summarizes these observations, saying, "Unless the LORD builds the house, those who build it labor in vain" (Ps. 127:1).

Although we who desire to be good and faithful people may give this phrase lip service, we generally do not act as if we believe it. However, all of us who have ever worked know of those days or those projects when, in spite of all our hard work and efforts, nothing gets done. We also all know of the opposite situation: days when, like magic, more than we could possibly have hoped for is accomplished. What is going on here?

One of the most basic assertions of our faith is that God is the Creator of heaven and earth. God creates. Not only that, but God creates out of nothing, a trick that not even the most type A person can manage. Unfortunately for most people, their understanding about God and creation stops there. This is because, I believe, most people of faith in the modern world are Deists. Deists see God as creating the universe and then receding to a far corner, pretty much leaving everything alone. In this view, God does the original creation, and people do all the subsequent work.

This interpretation of creation is not the theological stance of our faith tradition. Rather, creation is not confined to the beginning of the world but also understood to be continuing: God is continuously creating. Every day when we wake up and still have a functioning brain, we would do well to thank God for continuing to sustain and create in us this useful organ. To put this theological assertion another way: God is active in salvation history; God is at work.

It is perhaps not surprising that many people don't seem to like this understanding about God. People reject the notion of God as some kind of micromanager of events, and indeed the concept of continuous creation does bring up many questions about how God is involved in the continuous creation of the world. To even begin to answer these questions would require a metaphysical reflection beyond the scope of this book. However, troubling as it may be, the whole of our tradition—and certainly the contemplative side of our tradition—confirms that "the word of God is living and active, sharper than any two-edged sword" (Heb. 4:12).

The implication of this assertion is quite simple and also, from the perspective of the normal operation of the church, revolutionary. In the realm of the world, and certainly in the realm of the church, when we ask the question *Who works?* the answer rings out loud and clear: God.

IMPLICATIONS FOR MINISTRY

What does this insight tell us about Solomon's story, about ministry, and about the practice of prayer?

Solomon began his ministry by asking something of God. He didn't ask to build a temple; he didn't ask for new projects or programs; he asked for understanding and discernment (1 Kings 3:9). He prayed that he could know what God would have him do. Thus when the Temple finally was built, Solomon understood that it was built not because of his great work ethic or his brilliant ministry skills; rather, it was built because God wanted it built and ordained that Solomon should build it. God did the work, and Solomon simply followed.

This understanding that God's creative action is at the heart of our work in the world is not our prevailing model of ministry. Several years ago at a nearby church, the senior pastor introduced me to a new staff member. Not only was I told the person's name, but I was also told that he was their "savior" because of all the wonderful work he was going to do at the church. I said that I was very happy to finally meet Jesus.

A few months later I stopped by that same church and noticed that this person was no longer listed on the staff directory. I asked the senior pastor what had happened. It turns out that the person had been fired because he had proved to be "lazy." The pastor told me that the person was hired to "do new programming related to bringing new people into the church, and this didn't happen." From Jesus to slacker in a few short months—quite a drop in status.

The current prevailing model of ministry is compulsive programming. Church leaders are hired to work lots of hours to create programs that will bring people into the church. If they are the type of people who are good at this, they are good ministers; if not, they are failures. People expect this programming to happen regardless of whether the leader can recruit volunteers to help or whether anyone wants the programs in the first place.

In this world of compulsive programming, creation out of nothing does not flow from a God whose loving power is the source of endless energy and work. Instead, it is the harried activity of anxious humans who fear being fired as a consequence of the wrath of a parent or senior pastor should their results be less than dramatic. There is another way to approach spiritual work, and if we look at the story of Solomon and the Temple, we can see it. From the perspective of spiritual leadership, the alternative model of work is the practice of creative prayer.

THE PRACTICE OF CREATIVITY

CREATIVE PRAYER PRACTICE takes many forms and styles (see appendix). We can begin by focusing on those creative things that we already do, such as art or cooking or administration or teaching; or, we can consciously engage in creative acts for the specific purpose of praying.

As with all prayer practices, the point of creative prayer is to engage our relationship with God and listen or look for what God is showing us. We begin our time of prayer by noting our intention to focus on God, and we then bring our attention to this task. Creative prayer may be joined with other practices such as *lectio divina* or praying in nature (see chapter 10).

Unfortunately most people are convinced that they are not artists. For a number of reasons their creative impulses have been stifled. Creative prayer unleashes the creativity that flows from God to us and out through our prayer time, a wonderful benefit of this practice.

Our church recently engaged in a community-wide project of praying with art. People first spent time in prayer envisioning what healing meant to them. They then had the opportunity to paint their images on a ceramic tile, which eventually was kiln-fired. Although many people declared that they weren't artists and couldn't paint (even saying this as they painted beautiful tiles!), the results of this activity were astounding. What emerged were over one hundred beautiful images of the healing power of God in people's lives.

When you as a spiritual leader begin to engage in creative prayer, you will experience the creative power of God moving in you and in the life of the community. The more you pray creatively, the more you notice creation happening all around. You become attuned to and aware of the Spirit as it moves over the waters (Gen. 1:2), giving form to the life surrounding you. As with all the practices, your self-understanding will be essential to organizational transformation. I've met many spiritual leaders who say they have no creativity, who believe this; and sure enough, nothing creative is happening in their church or ministry.

In addition to times of creative prayer practice, another way you can engage creativity is through the appreciation of art. Take time to be involved with the arts. Look at paintings and other art forms, go to the movies, listen to music, spend time with artists. Although we are all capable of creativity, there certainly are some people who have this as a primary gift. The more you enjoy such people and their work, the more you can see with their eyes and hear with their ears. This too can foster your discernment of God's creative power as it moves in your community.

CREATIVITY, COMMUNITY, AND WORK

The most amazing thing about the healing-images tile project was how long people remained after church to paint tiles. Although we enjoy a wonderful and lively coffee hour, by the time an hour has passed, the church is usually empty. On the day we painted tiles at church (we also painted them at the local health clinic), members were still painting three hours after church services had ended.

I believe that people and communities long to create because we long for God. When God speaks through the prophet and says, "See, I am making all things new" (Rev. 21:5), God is speaking of creativity, and we all know how much we love new things. However, as with individuals, communities have often lost touch with the creative impulse.

One task of the spiritual leader is to reawaken this impulse and to allow the work of God to flourish in communal life. Just as with individuals, there are numerous ways to engage a group in creative prayer. Church music and educational programs offer natural starting places. Leaders need only teach and remind people that these are prayer activities and not just work.

Another major area for creative practice is worship, perhaps the most critical area to focus on when moving the community from a secular work model to a creative prayer model. I cannot say this more clearly or strongly: the leader must worship in worship. The more you engage in creative prayer, the more you will be able to relax in the worship setting. God will show up to create the worship experience. You do not need to work to make it happen.

Designing worship is not secular work; it is creative prayer. When a worship team begins to reflect upon the worship experience, discerning how God is present in worship, that team can design worship experiences that accentuate God's presence and foster people's awareness of this presence. In the story of Solomon, once the Temple building was complete—made according to the creative wisdom given to Solomon—the glory of God appeared in the Temple (2 Chron. 7:1). Solomon didn't need to create the experience or presence of God by his own effort.

As community members begin to see and understand the creative power of God in their midst, they become more open to listening for and following that power. They begin to let go of programming for its own sake—activity that exists so they can feel that the church is "doing something." This movement of work and energy from God to us rather than the other way around more accurately reflects our appropriate relationship to our Creator. Remember, we are followers of Jesus, not the other way around.

OUT OF NOTHING

One of the first—and often most strenuous—objections to running a church from the perspective of prayer is that "nothing will get done." This comment reflects the toxic work model. I guess people believe God is a real slacker, although certainly the evidence refutes this notion. In fact, if we consider the overabundance and diversity of life on our planet, it appears that God works much more than God has to. Our own understanding of God's ability to create and work is so impoverished and limited, we appear to think that engaging in the life of understanding and discernment, as Solomon did, will produce no results.

My experience is exactly the opposite. I have found in my own life and ministry that prayer produces more work than we can possibly handle. However, from the perspective of the life of prayer, I do not experience this work as toxic and overbearing. Instead, it is a yoke whose burden is easy and light (Matt. 11:30).

In a church where creative prayer runs the work of the community, it is easy to find volunteers and simple to design programs that work. People focus not on the activities themselves but rather on the risen Christ at the heart of the community. In this model, spiritual leaders are not compulsive overworkers; rather, they are grounded prayers. Furthermore, people are not quite so worried about filling their emptiness with stuff to do because the prayer life of the community has filled them with God, which is what they wanted in the first place.

SEVEN

SPEAKING AND WRITING
The Word and Our Words

TRAVELING COMPANION
Jesus

They asked [Jesus], "Teacher, we know that you are right in what you say and teach, and you show deference to no one, but teach the way of God in accordance with truth."

—*Luke 20:21*

Do not worry about how you are to speak or what you are to say; for what you are to say will be given to you at that time; for it is not you who speak, but the Spirit of your Father speaking through you.

—*Matthew 10:19-20*

e tend to underestimate speech. We forget that most everything we do or think, our relationships, and our work lives are mediated by words. Of course, this forgetting results from the omnipresence of words. We cannot imagine a world without language; in fact, we cannot imagine without the word *imagine*, and so we take speech for granted.

Everything I have discussed so far has been discussed using words: discernment, work, and prayer all come to us through the medium of speech. Thus it is perhaps not surprising that "in the beginning was the Word" (John 1:1). Even God is wrapped in, comprises, exists in speech.

The contemplative tradition understands speech as the method by which the unspoken experience of union with God is brought into the world, however imperfectly, and shared with others. All the great mystics have said that it is impossible to describe God or the experience of God. At the same time, they have striven to make their experiences known to others as a way of encouraging them in their own quest for a relationship with the divine.

Thus one cannot talk about spiritual leadership without reflecting upon words and prayer with words: written words, spoken words. We can see this deep connection when we look at all the great spiritual leaders of the Bible: they were sent by God to speak. Moses spoke to Pharaoh; the prophets spoke to kings; Jesus spoke to the crowds, the leaders of his time; he himself is the Word.

This chapter explores the intimate connection between words and spiritual leadership, between words and prayer.

WORDS AND TRUTH

In the Bible, words that come from God are associated with the truth. In Jesus' great speech toward the end of John's Gospel, he makes the remark "Sanctify them in the truth; your word is truth" (John 17:17). Jesus himself reinforces this connection between word and truth because he is both Word and Truth (John 1:14; John 14:6). As Jesus lived his ministry, he spoke to many people; the words he spoke were true and thus had great power. They had power to heal (Luke 7:7), to enlighten (John 8:12), to change lives (Luke 5:10), even to change religion (Matt. 12:12). Since Jesus has given us this example, it is useful to reflect upon the nature of words, both spoken and written, within the organizations that claim to follow Jesus.

A classic description of pastoral leadership names three components or functions to its practice: the priestly, the pastoral, and the prophetic. In this system, the latter two involve speech and are recognized as somewhat at odds, or at least existing in a kind of creative tension. The pastoral dimension invokes comforting, "nice" speech, while the prophetic aspect requires the confrontational speaking of hard truths.

Several generations of church leaders have been reared on this view of leadership with, I would suggest, disastrous results. The problem with this system of classification is that pastoral speech can quickly degenerate into false speech that avoids full assessment of reality; prophetic speech is either avoided altogether out of fear, reserved for angry confrontations, or, perhaps most commonly, consigned to the realm of declarations about people whose behavior is disliked— prophetic speech used to criticize others.

Because an organization follows in the footsteps of its leaders, churches accustomed to this pattern of speaking have tended to become places where within the tribe of church members the full truth is rarely spoken, while the members of the tribe feel free to speak all sorts of critical "truths" about those outside the tribe. This sort of codependent arrangement is thoroughly nonscriptural; as Jesus tells us, even sinners love their friends (Luke 6:32); certainly it does not follow the example of Jesus, whose enemies even recognized that he would speak and teach rightly and show no partiality but truly teach the way of God (Luke 20:21).

Speech that flows out of the life of prayer cannot be falsely divided into pastoral speech and prophetic speech. Speech that flows out of the life of prayer is speech that is true. It is both loving and confrontational; it enters into the life of a fallen world to both challenge that world and transform that world. If the speech of the church does not differ from the speech of the world, then the Word is not present, and the organization that calls itself the church is no church at all.

"With a Word"

To understand this issue of true speech and its relationship to prayer and the spiritual life, I want to look at scriptural examples that illustrate what a word from God does for those who encounter it. In Isaiah 50:4 we are told, "The Lord GOD has given me the tongue of a teacher, that I may know how to sustain the weary with a word." Then in Matthew 8:16 we hear the following about Jesus: "That evening they brought to him many who were possessed with demons; and he cast out the spirits with a word, and cured all who were sick."

In these examples two powerful things happen "with a word." First, those who are weary or sick are healed and sustained. They become better; they are transformed. The image of God that lies within people is more fully uncovered as they come into contact with God through words. Second, evil spirits are cast out. That which is fallen is defeated and sent away.

Notice that these two activities are not separate and distinct from each other, which is the message we get from the pastoral/prophetic speech divide. Rather, these actions are intimately connected. The process of removing evil and uplifting the person who is weary as a result of evil are two sides of a single coin. Unfortunately many people do not understand this connection. They are not necessarily in their churches to change and be healed; instead, they are often in church simply to reinforce their habits and receive assurance that God loves them anyway.

The task of the spiritual leader is to foster the community's ability to listen to "a word." This model of ministry, patterned on spiritual direction, can replace the pastor/ prophet model. In this model, a leader, through personal prayer, begins to listen for the word of God and then speaks it into the community.

"Speaking a word" is direct speech that lives in the present moment. By contrast, most speech in the church is abstract, especially sermons. Even when the preacher makes an effort to be *relevant*, the great buzzword in ministry, the words still hover above the real life of the community hearing the message. Ministers gravitate to abstractions because they aren't threatening. Abstractions don't spur people to action, force them to reflect upon themselves, or initiate change.

I know of more than one pastor who has changed churches because she or he simply got tired of preaching about certain issues—social justice, for example—while the congregation politely listened, nodded their heads, and ignored them. In the Gospel stories of Jesus we see that he used words in a different manner. When he encountered someone and spoke to him or her, his words were either very particular and direct, or he spoke in parables so that people had to listen and reflect upon what he said. His words could not be ignored.

For example, when Jesus spoke to the woman at the well (John 4:1-42), he did not talk generally about adultery or being a social outcast; no, Jesus told the woman everything she had ever done (John 4:39). He spoke directly into her life and circumstance. This directness is what gives the "word" power. Jesus' speech could not be ignored because its truth brought the power of God into the situation he was addressing. This is what good spiritual direction does: it speaks of the direction of the Spirit in the life of the person and community.

Praying with Words

A spiritual leader is one who knows the power of the Word. Thus PRAYING WITH WORDS, the practice of coming to hear and know the movement of the living Word, is essential for the work of the leader. There are numerous ways to be engaged in this practice (see appendix). Words are of course part of every prayer practice; even silent prayer uses a word that grounds you! In addition, it is helpful to regularly and intentionally engage in prayer with the written word.

Journaling and other written reflective prayers, such as the conversation with God, serve us well as we seek to hear and understand the power of writing and praying. In these practices, over time, we begin to hear another voice in the midst of the usual voice that crowds our mind.

In our culture "hearing voices" carries a negative connotation, and I am not talking about becoming psychotic. However, modern psychology understands that there are indeed many different "voices" in our mind. There are the voices of our parents, our teachers, other significant adults in our life; and there is the voice of God.

Because we tend to think of all the voices as our own, we habitually ignore God's voice, a voice we often perceive as telling us we "should" do something: we should take better care of ourselves; we should pray more; we should give up some bad habit. Attaching a "should" to this voice makes it unhelpful and often negative; this harmful process occurs because religious education often instills a large dose of guilt as part of faith. Thus we know we should be better people, but we aren't; so we feel bad, but we don't change, in part because we resent God for making us feel guilty. Hearing the word of God through this filter of guilt and shame results in a kind of perverted spiritual direction.

Prayer with words undermines this negative cycle of guilt and ignoring, and it helps us to hear the word of God in a new way, a way that is both loving and a call to change and growth. When we write down our reflections we are like the woman at the well. We hear Jesus telling us of our whole life and offering us living water too wonderful to turn down.

When you become practiced in hearing the Word of truth in your own life in a manner that is uplifting, challenging, and positive, you can then move on to help your community hear the Word in the same way.

Speaking What Is Most Helpful

Someone once described to me his theory of "least helpful speech." Based on his observation, people are least likely to tell someone what would actually be most helpful for the person to hear. I recently had a conversation with a friend who knew nothing about this theory but proceeded to provide an example that pointed to its truth. My friend had noticed a pattern of behavior in someone which she considered harmful to the woman. My friend asked, "Should I tell her?" Even though telling this person about her habit would be helpful, it was probably the last thing anyone was going to tell her.

A genuine spiritual leader reverses this trend and begins to speak that which is most helpful on a regular basis. In general there are four interconnected areas of speech at your disposal as a leader, and written prayer practices can be used in all of these areas. The four areas are: (1) speaking a helpful word into the community; (2) speaking about group discernment; (3) teaching about the spiritual life and life of prayer; and (4) training other leaders to speak a word.

Speaking a Helpful Word into the Community

Speaking a helpful word grows out of the personal practice of hearing a word from God. The questions you need to ask are *What does this community really need to hear? What would Jesus say to this community?* Awesome questions like these are not answered in isolation. Through individual and group practices of prayer, you begin to hear whatever God is speaking into the community already and then offer that word to the community.

One simple example of this practice at my current church involved an issue related to the format for our Sunday school classrooms. The tradition in our church called for individual classrooms, divided by age level, much like a traditional school setting. This plan worked in the day when lots of kids were enrolled in each grade level. But in spite of declining enrollment, the church continued to have individual classrooms for each age level.

Over the years I had heard expressions of discontent and frustration about small class sizes, yet each year we would ignore these comments and continue with separate classes. Finally one year I suggested a multiage classroom format. To me this was the helpful word that needed to be spoken to the committee. The result of this suggestion was quite positive. Everyone was excited to try the new format; the complaints and frustrations vanished; and this system has worked well ever since. This was indeed the word that led in the direction of the Spirit.

Speaking about Group Discernment

The previous example also illustrates the fact that speaking a word often gives voice to group discernment. As the church organization becomes used to the practice of discernment, it also becomes used to hearing the word of God in its midst. Writing these discernments can be useful for the community as a whole.

Sometimes I invite everyone in worship to spend some time in prayer and then write their reflections on a particular topic or issue. This might be a theological reflection. We once spent three Sundays reflecting and writing on the topics of confession, repentance, and forgiveness. The reflection might be more practical in nature: on the direction of the church, for example. I collect these writings and share them with the whole community, with the church board, or both. Praying over these writings then becomes a source of community discernment, and our leadership is asked to speak about what they are hearing in these written words.

The leaders in this situation speak of the general themes and directions that emerge out of the reflections. This role is critical because at first people have a hard time even hearing what their own observations are telling them. Although it may seem obvious in retrospect, the thematic similarities in a group discernment are not always clear to the members of the group. A practiced leader who can speak these words into the community offers valuable assistance.

Teaching about the Spiritual Life and Life of Prayer

Moving a church from a secular organizational model to a spiritual one represents an enormous change, and the transition can be challenging. Numerous questions will arise about organizational structure, the nature and source of the prayer practices, the point of the change, and so forth. People will wonder if you have become a Buddhist or New Age practitioner; they will wonder what happened to traditional committees—even if they find they enjoy not going to boring committee meetings!

In the midst of such transition, teaching becomes a critical role for you as a leader. Luckily leaders of the church have many opportunities for such teaching. Sermons, teaching times at the beginning of meetings, newsletter articles, and private discussions all become moments to explain the nature of the spiritual life to the community.

Here is one more area where your personal practice is so vital. Quite frankly, explaining the spiritual life is hard, especially to those who have no experience with it. If leaders are not practicing prayer, the task becomes even more challenging. Often such unpracticed explanations sound trite or even bizarre: "Well, it's not about doing anything; it's just about being." Only when you are familiar with prayer in your own life can you teach others.

However, once you can begin to explain the life of prayer to your community, the benefits are tremendous. This is because everyone who is in a church really does, at some level, want to encounter God; they just need direction and reassurance. Good teaching can provide this direction and can encourage the process of allowing Jesus to become present and active in the church.

Training Other Leaders to Speak a Word

A senior pastor discussed with me his need to speak some difficult words to a staff member. Quite honestly, he was scared to do it. "What if he shoots me?" the man asked me, only half in jest. This incident points to both the importance and the difficulty of the work described in this chapter. The entire leadership of the church, and indeed as many people in the community as possible, must embrace the notion that church is about seeing, hearing, and following the living Word in the midst of the community.

Fortunately this senior pastor didn't give in to his fear. He did have the discussion with the staff member. Furthermore, he used a written prayer practice as a tool for the conversation: he created four questions that he wanted this staff member to pray and reflect upon. What happened in this exchange showed me how much we underestimate

God. Not only did no violence ensue, but in fact the opposite occurred; the staff person embraced the feedback and the written questions with openness and enthusiasm.

This work of training other leaders to hear and respond to the Word so that they too can speak a word to others is critical to transforming the church. Whether it is through your direct work of teaching and training, as in the example above, or suggesting that others seek spiritual direction, or promoting training opportunities, leaders would do well to encourage other leaders to pray with words.

And though this work is challenging, we must persevere. The Bible is full of people who claimed they could not speak, and certainly not the word of God. However, as the scripture states, "Do not worry about how you are to speak or what you are to say; for what you are to say will be given to you at that time; for it is not you who speak, but the Spirit of your Father speaking through you" (Matt. 10:19-20).

As we pray with words, we can more clearly hear the Word that is Christ speaking to us. And, like the people in the upper room in Acts 1:13, we can be empowered by our experiences with the Spirit to speak God's word to a fallen world.

EIGHT

INCARNATING PRAYER
The Body and the Spiritual Life

TRAVELING COMPANION
Lazarus

*[Jesus] cried with a loud voice, "Lazarus, come out!"
The dead man came out, his hands and feet bound
with strips of cloth, and his face wrapped in a cloth.
Jesus said to them, "Unbind him, and let him go."*

—*John 11:43-44*

hristianity's relationship with our physical bodies has not been healthy. Unfortunately our faith has tended to be spiritualized in a way that ignores and neglects the body and even regards it as evil. These attitudes persist despite the fact that Jesus came to us in a body; although sometimes I think there is a general belief that the only reason for this was so that his body could be destroyed.

This poor relationship with our physical selves has serious ramifications in terms of leadership. Pastors are sicker and more depressed than the general population. Indeed, a serious clergy health-care crisis looms as a whole cohort of ill pastors moves toward retirement age. Furthermore, pornography addiction and other sexual dysfunctions, conditions with obvious connections to the body, plague church leadership.

Something is deeply wrong with this situation. How can we talk within the church about a Jesus who healed people, who made bodies well, and yet have church leaders whose bodies are sick and getting sicker all the time? Spiritual leadership, leadership informed by the Spirit working through people, cannot function within this twisted state of affairs. If we call the Holy Spirit the Lord and the giver of life, then those who proclaim such a teaching must themselves be evidence of this same life-giving Spirit.

We dare to call the church "the body," the manifestation of the body of Christ on earth. And this is not the beaten, dead body of Jesus on the cross. Rather, this is the resurrected body of Christ—a body that has attained victory over death. Again, how can we make this claim for ultimate health and healing while showing the world sick and broken leaders?

Incarnating prayer—praying with our bodies—is and must be an essential component of our discussion of spiritual leadership. Our negative relationship with our bodies requires a sort of antileader to help with this conversation. The previous chapters cited figures from the Bible who could be obviously identified as leaders. Here, however, I turn to a far less likely leadership figure: Lazarus.

THE GOSPEL IN HIS BODY

There are two stories in the Gospels about a man named Lazarus (in Luke 16 and John 11–12). These don't appear to be the same person, and yet there are interesting similarities to the two stories. Neither Lazarus speaks, and both of them die after having been quite unwell. Thus their bodies and bodily conditions are in many ways the focus of their stories. We do not hear about their faith, about their theological opinions, even about their feelings regarding Jesus. Rather, they bear in their bodies the fallen condition of the world; they are sick, and that is all we know.

Then we find out what happens to them after death. In both stories the men's bodily condition is restored or relieved. In one, we hear that Lazarus now rests comfortably with Abraham (Luke 16:23); we presume that he has all he needs on a bodily level. In the other, more famous story, Lazarus is raised from the dead and unbound (John 11:44). Neither story focuses on the mind of Lazarus, on faith—the center of so many healing stories—but rather on bodily restoration.

Neither Lazarus is a leader in the true sense of the word. He doesn't lead people directly. Yet we hear that a "great crowd" came, "not only because of Jesus but also to see Lazarus, whom he had raised from the dead" (John

12:9). Lazarus becomes a leader because of what he embodies: he is the bodily manifestation of the gospel. The good news is that his illness, which all supposed would lead to death (John 11:4), is gone, and his body has been made well. Lazarus leads by example, an example put forth so that we might believe (John 11:15). In this sense Lazarus provides an example of spiritual leadership. What can we learn from him?

A Confused Theology

Jesus' words about taking up your cross (Matt. 16:24; Mark 8:34; and Luke 9:23) have, unfortunately, been the source of a highly confused and negative theology of embodiment. The common interpretation of these sayings could be paraphrased as: "If it hurts, it must be of God." Thus wives have been counseled to stay with abusive husbands; children have endured corporal punishment; and spiritual leaders have embraced being worked to death—all because these activities are clearly unpleasant and therefore must be a sign of the "cross" that we all must endure in order to be holy.

While this theology might be effective for controlling people or keeping them in a perpetual state of guilt and fear, it is certainly not a life-giving theology of resurrection. I believe this theology has had more to do with the decline of the modern church than any other single cause.

From the perspective of the spiritual life, taking up one's cross is indeed of great consequence, but it has nothing to do with endlessly enduring senseless suffering. Instead, this admonition to be transformed by the symbol of our faith points in two other directions. First, we are to embrace the suffering that comes with living in a fallen world; and, second, we are to allow the death of our own self-centered lives that we may live into the life abundant that God offers us.

The Cross symbolizes the endless suffering meted out by a world that is blinded by sin. Because the world did not know Jesus (1 John 3:1), it crucified him. So too as we live in this world, we meet suffering just by being here. This is the suffering of broken relationships, of sickness, of death and loss. Most of the time we seek to avoid suffering, either by getting away from it or by ignoring it. I'm sure that most people who saw the Lazarus with dogs licking his sores (Luke 16:21) simply turned their heads and walked away. Taking up the cross calls us to embrace rather than ignore the suffering of this world. Taking up the cross awakens a compassion and a healing power in us that in turn kindles desire to bring the kingdom into our midst. Without Lazarus's death there would have been no new life.

The Cross is also a sign that our fallen selves must die, the selves that look at the world only in terms of what it can do for us. The practice of prayer really concerns the death of this self. Every time we sit in silence, pray the Jesus Prayer, or do any prayer practice, we are taking up our cross and committing ourselves to God's life, not our own. However, we must remember that is the good (see Gen. 1) life of the original creation, not a life of death and self-mutilation. When Lazarus encountered the life that Jesus had to offer, he was unbound.

I once heard of a church that had 1.2 million dollars in the bank. Yet at the same time their church building was falling apart, and they hired one seriously ill pastor after another. This church embodied the confused theology of the Cross. They embraced sickness and death rather than health and life, and it showed in both the bodies of their leaders and the body of their church structure. Spiritual leadership embraces a different theology of embodiment— the embodiment of healing, the embodiment of "your kingdom come. Your will be done, on *earth* as it is in heaven" (Matt. 6:10, emphasis added).

EMBODIED PRAYER

As with all prayer practices, embodied prayer is about awareness and listening, in this case to the body. If you are a spiritual leader committed to praying within the body that God gave you, begin by paying attention to your body. Ask yourself: *What is the state of my body? Is it healthy or ill? Do I love the body that God gave me or do I hate it? What is the nature of my relationship to bodily activities— to eating, sleeping, sex, exercise?*

You may find these radical, new, and difficult questions. It may be that years of ignoring your body has led to serious problems that will take a while to repair. These questions need to be asked with kindness and compassion rather than condemnation, and it may be that seeking outside help, medical or psychological, will be part of the healing process.

Perhaps you will find it hard to consider this sort of health inventory as prayer. It doesn't sound like familiar prayer practices, such as silent prayer or scripture prayer, yet paying attention to the holy temple God gave you to live in constitutes a prayer practice if done in relationship with God. To aid with this attention to God, try combining this health inventory with an examen. When you look at your current state of embodiment, what is "of God" and what is not?

For example, is it life-giving to work in a way that prevents giving attention to your children, as many church leaders do? More than one church leader has told me how chilling it was to hear from an adult child that church had hurt their parent-child relationship. Using the examen with all your bodily relationships can turn your awareness to God's desire for your embodied life.

Again the example of Lazarus (both of them!) can be instructive. When the Lazarus of the Lucan story (Luke 16:22) arrived in God's kingdom, what happened to him? This was the moment he encountered God face-to-face. Did his poor health continue? Did he get more sores? Was he told that this was his cross and he just had to suck it up and bear it? No, he was healed and comforted. Thus as you pray with your body, pay attention to your own thoughts and feelings and prejudices regarding your state of health or illness. Watch to see if you really believe that God wants you to be sick and broken. If you do believe this, how can you square this belief with story upon story of Jesus healing those whom he encountered?

Once you have begun to pay attention to your body and realize that this attention is part of your prayer life, you can expand your repertoire of BODY PRAYER to include specific prayer practices (see appendix). Thus breath prayers, movement prayers, as well as various walking prayers (see chapter 10) are all bodily prayers that can be helpful as you seek to incarnate the gospel in your bodily self.

LEADERSHIP AND THE BODY

What are the ramifications of body prayer for leadership? Christian spiritual leaders need to make an important decision regarding their understanding of the faith: is

Christianity only about getting to heaven, or does it also have significant implications for life on earth? Essentially this question addresses embodiment, and I raise it because, perhaps unconsciously, Christianity is often presented as a tool for the afterlife with little to say about our incarnate beings.

Indeed if our faith only prepares us for heaven, then our bodies matter little. But if faith requires following a resurrected Christ who lives and acts now, whose will be done on earth as God restores a fallen creation, moving us to the promised land, then Christian spiritual leadership is an embodied leadership. And praying with our bodies helps us to follow God here on earth and not simply hope that we get to meet God later on and far away.

Several years ago I served on the staff of the Youth Ministry and Spirituality Project. This project promoted spiritual leadership within youth ministry. ABC news covered part of our work in a story on youth and spirituality. In order to get footage for the story, a producer from ABC came to one of our weeklong events. ABC had also spent time with many other youth-related religious groups and organizations. At the end of the week, the producer made a revealing comment. She said that at most of the other events, what happened in front of the kids and what happened behind the scenes was often very different, that what was being said to the youth wasn't being practiced by the staff. For example, adults might talk about the love of Christ to the kids but then treat one another badly during staff meetings. What impressed her about our project was that we were trying to live out, with one another, what we were teaching the youth. In other words, we talked about praying with the young people, and at staff meetings we prayed together. We talked about the importance of listening and working together as a team, and we practiced these skills with one another. In short, we embodied what we were saying.

Most of us know the phrase "actions speak louder than words." This is a statement about embodiment. If we as leaders believe that our faith is about God being present in our world here and now, then, like Lazarus, we must embody that gospel, embody that good news. As we learn to pray with our bodies, we become living examples who can encourage our communities to embrace an embodied gospel.

BODY PRAYER IN COMMUNITY

One way to understand, and then practice, body prayer in community is through hospitality. Hospitality fundamentally relates to the body. When we welcome people into our homes, when we greet them, sit them down in a comfortable place, feed them, take care of their bodily needs, we are paying attention to their bodies and welcoming them with the loving generosity with which God welcomes us.

In the spiritual tradition, hospitality has been esteemed as one of the great communal spiritual practices. This status stems directly from the Gospel story about those who cared for the king and those who did not (Matt. 25:31-46). If we look at the list of actions given as signs of those who cared for and welcomed the coming of God, we see that all relate to our embodied selves: feeding, providing clothes, visiting, caring for the ill. None of these activities pertains only to the mind: correct doctrine, religious habit, or belief, for instance. Rather, it is through hospitality, especially for those in need, that we welcome and acknowledge God.

In your role as a leader, reflect on the hospitality of your community. How do you welcome people? How do you care for people? How do people feel when they arrive at your church?

Unfortunately, leaders often get the clearest picture of performance in these areas through negative examples. I once led a retreat at a center where my coleader was yelled at not once but several times by a stressed-out worker in the house where we were staying. This lady obviously was in no position to offer us hospitality—a situation all too common in church settings. Grumpy grounds workers, overloaded secretaries, angry volunteers inhabit more churches than we are willing to admit. If church leaders can begin to understand bodily prayer in terms of hospitality, then there are many ways to begin encouraging the community to pray with its collective body.

First, give attention to the church building itself. Taking the example of the dilapidated church with a million dollars in the bank, we can imagine that if the leadership had focused on hospitality, they would have used some funds to turn the church building into a welcoming space. So, ask yourself, *When people enter the physical space of this church, what do they see? Is there a place to sit and gather? Is there nice artwork on the walls, a warm, welcoming environment?*

One of the best changes we have made at our church was creating a lovely place to sit in the narthex, replacing a cramped space with only one long pew to sit on. This modification has generated more compliments from strangers and nonchurch members than almost anything else we have done in several years. Why? Because when people come into our church for funerals, weddings, or special events, they feel welcomed and comfortable and thus experience, even if in a small way, the gospel.

The next place to turn your attention regarding hospitality is ongoing ministries that create an environment in which the Spirit moves freely. Such ministries typically include prayer chains, Stephen Ministries and other healing efforts, quilting or prayer shawl groups. Church leaders need to consciously make the core meaning of these ministries clear. These are not just things "to do" (especially not in a compulsive manner); rather, they are prayer practices about caring for bodies.

Finally, look at worship and the question of how people feel in church. Many churches are uptight places. People come to worship feeling scared and tense, worried that their children will misbehave or that someone will judge them or their behavior. These feelings embody a negative gospel, not the gospel of Jesus, who welcomes us home with love and joy.

Honestly assess the bodily experience of people in your worshiping community. If they are scared and anxious, then ask what is causing those feelings and why is the church not embodying the emotions of joy, happiness, and relaxation.

One of the best ways to begin to embody the gospel in community is for people to know one another's joys and concerns and to pray for one another. One focus of spiritual leadership can be addressing how this kind of sharing and prayer can be incorporated into worship and the overall life of the congregation.

Another way to pray into the body of the community is to talk about our bodies! People often try to avoid this topic at all costs. As a spiritual leader in your community you can demonstrate willingness to take on the subject of our bodies: how we do or do not pray with them, treat them well, appreciate them, see them as gifts from God. The community will begin to relax then and be open to regarding their embodiment in a spiritual light.

Prayers related to the body often come down to simple petitions for an illness to go away. While there is nothing wrong with such prayer, to pray only in this manner is very limited. God gave us bodies to use, to marvel at, to enjoy, and to pray with. Furthermore, God came to us in the form of Jesus, an embodied human, to unbind us and set us free. As we pray into our embodiment as a community, we create spaces where the kingdom of God is experienced and made real. This is what Lazarus knew in his body, and it is what leaders are called to make real in their own bodies and to help make real in our life together.

NINE

WALKING TOWARD GOD
The Journey Made Visible

TRAVELING COMPANION
Peter

*As [Jesus] walked by the Sea of Galilee, he saw two
brothers, Simon, who is called Peter, and Andrew his
brother, casting a net into the sea—for they were
fishermen. And he said to them, "Follow me,
and I will make you fish for people."
Immediately they left their nets and followed him.*
—Matthew 4:18-20

ollow me." One of the most compelling sentences in the Bible. Two words, when spoken by Jesus, create a sense of power and mystery and awe. To follow is to enter into the unknown, to give your life over to another. We rarely want to do this. Yet at the same time it is exactly what we desire: to be led into a better place, a better world, a better life. This is what Jesus offered to these simple fishermen, and amazingly enough, they took the offer. Their lives would never be the same.

Journey and movement are central metaphors in the spiritual life. The recognition that humans are separated from God by sin and that our life of faith involves the mutual movement of humans toward God and God toward us is absolutely fundamental to our understanding of life on earth. And we see this drama of movement beginning in the short passage from Matthew. Jesus moves toward these men and then invites them to move toward him.

The spiritual life concerns more than an individual's movement toward God. As we see in this passage, Jesus invites these men on a journey that includes others, and it is a missional journey. One reason behind the difficulty in making the transition from individual spiritual practice to spiritual leadership is our conception of the spiritual life as highly individualized. We typically view the journey to God as "my" journey. I do the practices, and it is too hard or messy or inconvenient to engage others in the journey.

Peter, whom we first meet here by the shore, is one of the pivotal figures of Christianity. Jesus certainly sets him on a journey, both an individual journey and a collective journey. The individual journey charts Peter's spiritual growth, a transformation employed and mirrored in the growth of the early church.

The previous chapters have discussed creating a praying community, a living spiritual organism. In describing this process of forming a praying organism, I have focused on the mind, the heart, the body of this collective being, led by God through those who have embraced the spiritual life. Yet this new creation is not meant to stagnate or to simply sit and serve itself. Too many churches exist in that state, like so many spiritual couch potatoes, and they finally die of inertia. Rather, this living entity is built to move, to journey through time and space, just as Jesus did, fishing for people, bringing the kingdom of God to those who need the good news.

Thus these last chapters highlight prayer practices that bring leaders and communities out into the world. These practices foster dynamic organizations that seek to serve those around them, demonstrating the love of God to all. In this chapter I will explain the walking prayer practices that embody the notion of journey as well as reflect on the historical unfolding of a spiritual community—a process similar to personal spiritual development. The biblical figure for this chapter is Peter, one who in his own life so beautifully demonstrates the transformative journey that is the encounter with Jesus.

PETER'S JOURNEY AND HISTORICAL UNFOLDING

A joke circulating on the Internet and around various religious institutions imagines a corporate personnel evaluation of the twelve disciples. In the tale, eleven out of the twelve flunk the evaluation. The only one who shows promise from the perspective of the corporate human resources folks is Judas. According to the evaluation, Peter's rating is especially poor—something we could predict from the Gospel witness!

If we were going to pick one person not to be the first pope, it would be Peter. He routinely says the wrong things, misunderstands the lessons, is called Satan by Jesus, and in his final act before the resurrection, denies Jesus three times (Matt. 26:75). Yet by the time we see him in Acts, having encountered the Spirit on the Day of Pentecost, he is giving eloquent speeches, having visions that lead to profound theological insights, and healing people just as Jesus did (see Acts 2:14; 10:13; 3:6). Looking back from this vantage point, we see that Jesus' original prediction, being fishers of people, had come true. Who would have known?

Embracing the whole story, we realize that Peter's life had a certain trajectory, a spiritual arc that, in spite of all the twists and turns, still bent itself gracefully toward its goal of church leadership. This constituted the historical movement of his life, his journey, and as he walked the streets of Galilee and Jerusalem with Jesus, this journey unfolded in the manner that God knew it would.

Throughout time different cultures and religions have wrestled with the issue of fate, or determinism. Posed in several ways, this question asks, *If God is all-knowing and exists in eternity, which includes all times, is our future already laid out for us?* In cultures and traditions that are very fatalistic, the answer has been yes: our fate is determined already and we have very little say in it. Other traditions have contended that free will plays a significant role and that our future is open to a number of possibilities depending on our choices.

Even within Christianity there have been different answers to this question, in part because it is a tricky one to answer! However, generally speaking, our faith has affirmed both God's determination of history and a role for our choices and actions in the unfolding of this history. Thus Peter could have chosen not to follow Jesus. His choice was important, and Jesus probably was pretty good at picking people who would follow him and thus knew how the future would unfold.

Given this "both/and" answer to the question of fate, the contemplative tradition says that the point of the life of prayer, relative to the issue of the future, is to fuse our choices with God's will such that we participate fully and seamlessly with the unfolding of God's salvation history. From this perspective, sin—our tendency to want to create our own future as if we are God—is regarded as resistance; it blocks the flow of God's will to salvation. While sin cannot ultimately be successful in thwarting God; it can cause a lot of turbulence and waste a lot of time and energy. Thus the more we pray into the journey that is our lives, the less resistance there is to the journey God has put before us, and the more we can love, enjoy, relish, and participate in that journey.

WHAT IS GOD DOING HERE?

Start the practice of walking prayer with the understanding that we and all the people around us in our time and place are already on a God-given quest. On a spiritual walk we sees people and communities not as static entities but as dynamic groups of people who are all moving together through time, much like being on an invisible moving walkway. Furthermore, this flow, this movement, is not random but has a trajectory as part of salvation history.

As a spiritual leader, you walk your community in prayer with the questions *What is God doing here? What is the journey that we are on together?* The practice of SLOW WALKING (see appendix) serves well for reflecting on this question. As you move slowly through space, you can allow your minds to settle and become clearer, opening to God's presence in your midst. To walk and pray also allows you to see the civic community around you. Who inhabits your community? What are the historical, economic, and social forces shaping your geographical area? What is God doing here?

As with all prayer practices, the examination of your journey begins with yourself and moves outward to the church. When my family and I arrived in Crookston, we had the almost comic experience of being asked repeatedly, "What are you doing here?" I suppose people from a small Midwestern town couldn't quite believe that a professional couple with lots of choices about places to live would choose to come there.

But I also think that this was indeed a spiritual question, God speaking to us through many different folks. This question encouraged me to look at myself as well as all the other people in the church and in the town and wonder, *What are we all doing here? Most importantly, what is God doing here?*

When you as a spiritual leader ask these questions and practice the prayer of journey, several shifts begin. First, you start to relax. As you pray and walk you notice your mind settling. You become less anxious and worried about the future. You move, and God moves with you. When you truly understand that God is unfolding history, you also realize that there is so much less for us to do. The creation of the kingdom is not in our hands! What a relief.

This relaxation can then lead to curiosity about just what God is doing. A childlike simplicity about what will happen next emerges. You expect something amazing will happen! When Jesus first recruited Peter he didn't tell him all that would happen to him. Jesus didn't lay out his agenda like a tour guide offering an all-expense-paid seven-day vacation to Hawaii. So it was that one day Peter found himself walking on water (Matt. 14:29). This is something he never would have predicted or imagined himself doing, yet this was where his spiritual journey led.

As you pray, walk, and move in time through your church and your town or city, remarkable change will happen as opportunities for ministry and mission come your way. If you are curious and open to these opportunities, you are able to see what God is putting right in front of your faces.

That recognition leads to the final result of the practice of journey: gaining the ability to respond to God's movement in history. What if Peter had not waited in the upper room as the disciples were instructed? What if he had said to himself, "Well, I'm the first pope. I'd better get to work. I've got lots to accomplish, lots of programs to run, no time to waste." Off he'd go, charging this way and that, and when the Holy Spirit descended in Jerusalem, he just happened to be trying, unsuccessfully, to run a revival in Athens. Oh well.

If you as a spiritual leader have faith that God moves in history, and thus in our lives, you can wait with openness and curiosity, alert to whatever God is doing. This practice allows you to respond to God's invitations, because you are there and present to receive them. The practice of walking and praying trains you to pay attention to the movements of God's Spirit and nurtures the ability to react freely when these movements present themselves. Because Peter did wait and pray in the upper room, he received the Holy Spirit and was able to deliver his great speech in response to the crowd; and when he was asked, "What should we do?" (Acts 2:37), he came up with an answer that generated a tremendous flow of people into the early church community. All this resulted from almost no "work" on Peter's part; rather, it simply required prayer and faithfulness on his journey with Jesus.

THE COMMUNAL JOURNEY

I often hear pastors and other spiritual leaders lament what is *not* happening in their churches. Usually this lament stems from anxiety spawned by the latest fad in church leadership, a preconceived notion about "growth," or some other cookie-cutter model of ministry. Rarely do I hear leaders ask, "What is God already doing in the particular history of this congregation?"

Like individuals, communities have histories and trajectories as well. Israel seemed destined to rise and fall in response to the faithfulness of the people. Exile was predicted by the prophets. So too it was predicted that in "the fullness of time" (Eph. 1:10) a Messiah would be born. Also, as with individuals, communities often ignore or fight against these trajectories based on judgments defined by their own ideas and agendas. In a classic example of this reality, the Jesus' disciples wanted him to be a typical earthly king rather than a spiritual messianic king. They had one vision of kingdom growth while God was at work with another plan.

Once you begin to pray into the journey of your community, you will develop, as the Serenity Prayer says, the courage to change the things that can be changed, accept the things that can't, and the wisdom to know the difference. You will not be so concerned about applying the latest techniques of ministry but more concerned about encouraging members of the community to become aware of their collective journey. Encouraging this awareness enables them to focus on where Jesus is leading them rather than on where he isn't going.

The LABYRINTH (see appendix) is a wonderful walking prayer practice that encourages awareness of journey with God. As it gained popularity in the Middle Ages, the labyrinth became one way to practice pilgrimage rather than make the journey to Jerusalem. It consists of three phases of movement: (1) going into the labyrinth and letting go of all that keeps us from connecting with God; (2) arriving at the center of the labyrinth, which represents the state of union with God; and (3) then leaving the labyrinth and returning to the world in a new way, accompanied by God.

When walking the labyrinth, maintain the attitude of pilgrimage. That means keeping the sense of not knowing exactly where you are going. A pilgrimage differs from a traveling vacation in that it always remains a bit out of one's control. God, not the traveler, is in charge of the quest. Each time you enter the labyrinth, you do not know exactly what you will find or how you will experience your time with God. This is a good thing. It robs you of your desire to control your spiritual journey.

Groups and communities will find the labyrinth an excellent practice. Of course, the challenge may be finding a labyrinth; however, there are an increasing number of them being built in churches and other locations, and portable ones can be set up in fellowship halls, gyms, or other large common spaces. As more people walk the labyrinth, the collective understanding of journey with God grows, and people become more open to knowing that God is working for some good purpose in the life of their community. The same three stages of relaxation, curiosity, and openness to a response occur in the church that is on a journey. The process allows the community to transform into one that is on "the Way" (Acts 9:2), just like the early church.

A MIND FOR MISSION

What are the results of prayer walking, of praying into the journey with God? One sign of this journey in a church body is the desire to be in mission. Most churches in America spend about 2 to 3 percent of their annual budget on mission, and most of that money goes outside their community to a denominational general mission fund.

Paradoxically, churches that pray a lot, that is, "do nothing" a lot, are communities that do a lot of mission work. This is because of God's calling to become fishers of people (Matt. 4:19). The mission field is ultimately where God leads us. However, when such mission work arises out of the life of prayer, it happens in a grace-filled and non-compulsive manner.

In the past five years, our church has undertaken about a dozen significant mission efforts in our community. These have been both direct efforts of the church and also efforts in the larger community in which church members have exercised significant leadership roles.

The mission efforts directly from the church usually began when a person came up to me and said something like, "It seems that God is calling me to do something about . . .". From there energy, money, and an activity emerged. The key ingredient in this birth is, I think, an open environment in which the Spirit can lead a group of people wherever God is calling them. The history of our community is allowed to unfold, and we simply watch as miracles occur all around us.

One of my favorite Peter stories is his response to the Transfiguration (Matt. 17:1-8; Mark 9:2-8; Luke 9:28-36). In the midst of this astounding revelation, Peter feels that perhaps the best response would be a small carpentry project (Mark 9:5). When we read this today, it seems rather foolish or, at best, a bit confused. Yet in many ways our own attempts to do ministry projects separate from the full light of God's revelation probably seem just as absurd. The practice of walking and praying, of fully immersing ourselves in the journey that God puts us on, offers the antidote to the disconnect between our work and God's work. If we are willing to embark upon this journey, we too will eventually find our way through the fog of our own confusion so that we may embrace the power and work of the Spirit in our midst.

TEN

PRAYING IN NATURE

Contemplation, Creation, and Leadership

TRAVELING COMPANION
Mary

She had a sister named Mary, who sat at the Lord's feet and listened to what he was saying.

—Luke 10:39

*M*any years ago I took a trip to the Badlands in South Dakota. I was there with the woman who is now my wife, and we were camping in the wilderness. With our tent perched upon a small mound of ancient earth, we set off to hike amid the beauty of this rugged terrain. I remember the greens of the grass, the strange whites and earth tones of the primeval mud formations, and the vast beauty of the sky.

At one point our conversation turned philosophical, and I spoke about my sense of being in the midst of a giant temple where God's presence was so obvious. I also imagined how a group of people might come to such a place and immediately build several church buildings where they would go to worship God, and from which they could begin to argue with one another about the "correct" understanding of God. And all the while, this incredible scene, now ignored, which practically shouted "God," would unfold all around them.

Neither the church building nor the church community exists in an isolated vacuum. Just as we are not disembodied spirits floating in search of our Creator but rather reside in physical bodies that are a part of our holy existence, so too our church communities and buildings do not exist separately from the creation that breaks into songs and praise for God (Ps. 98:4). Rather, our communities are embedded within a natural world of which we are an integral part.

Our prayer life and our life as leaders draw us out into the world in service and mission. As part of this work, relationship with the world created by God can be a life-giving focus not only for us but for our community. This chapter explores not only how leaders pray in and with nature but also how to focus leadership on our interaction with the world God has given us to steward.

The biblical figure for our exploration is another unlikely leader: Mary, Lazarus's sister. This is the woman who decided to sit at the feet of Jesus and listen to his teachings rather than clean house. She was someone whose focus on Jesus was so strong she essentially forgot all else. Her attention paved the way for the dramatic event of her brother's resurrection. Mary sought to gaze at God through all else, and it is this deep gaze—a type of looking we can employ when we pray with nature—that allows us to see and hear the teachings God has for us. However, in order for us to do this, we must overcome certain obstacles in our relationship with God's creation.

ANOTHER PROBLEMATIC RELATIONSHIP

Like our relationship with our bodies, our relationship with nature—both actual and theological—is a difficult one. Unlike the psalmist who could pen Psalm 104, in which all the earth stands as testimony to the incredible power, beauty, and wisdom of God, we find ourselves increasingly at odds with the natural world. I would like to describe three impediments to spiritual leadership, all of which can be healed by praying in nature. These impediments are (1) the theological understanding of dominion; (2) the problem with "natural theology"; and (3) our alienation from creation.

Unfortunately the biblical instruction to "have dominion" over and "subdue" nature (Gen. 1:28) has often been interpreted to mean a mindless sort of domination in which people regard nature as something to plunder. According to this view, nature is an inanimate object standing outside ourselves for us to control. In many ways, this view is responsible for the sorts of environmental crises we see unfolding around us.

Yet, in the Bible, dominion is related to kingship, and any discussion of kingship revolves around the question of whether the kingdom is "of God." For example, Isaiah criticizes a kingdom that has cared for its land and its people improperly (for example, Isaiah 5). Similarly, we can see that a "kingdom" that treats the earth badly, whose activity results in polluted air and water or poor sanitation, is not a kingdom that has exercised good dominion.

The second issue, related to "natural theology," arises because our faith is grounded in the written Word. Because of this, there has been a tendency to see nature, and God speaking through nature, as a pagan counterpart to true faith. So-called "natural theology" has been criticized as un-Christian. The problem with this criticism has been the failure to differentiate between God speaking through nature and nature being God. The latter view is not substantiated by our faith, but scripture proudly proclaims that God speaks through the world God created.

Finally, technological, industrialized society and its way of life have caused people to become increasingly removed from the natural world. Throughout the world, but particularly in the industrialized nations, more and more people live in cities or suburbs and work in cubicles or factories, settings where they are completely alienated from creation.

This alienation has caused people to believe, however unconsciously, that humans exist independently from the natural world. We seem to exist just fine without it, because, for example, food comes from a box rather than from the earth. Why should we pay the earth much thought? However, we are beginning to realize the substantial price we pay for this alienation as our collective sense of isolation, despair, and depression grows.

These three tendencies, which exist to varying degrees within every church community, can result in a congregation that pays little attention to the natural world or its own relationship to nature. Let us now look at these issues through Mary's eyes and see what her interaction with Jesus reveals about how we might go about praying in creation.

MARY'S VIEW

When we observe Mary sitting at the feet of Jesus, talking to Jesus about her brother, weeping in front of him so that he is moved to sorrow (John 11:33), we witness a relationship with God. We also witness a kingdom of God that is the antithesis of domination and alienation. Mary exists in a close, intimate, loving communion with Jesus. We can learn from examining this relationship because we claim that Jesus offers the clearest view of what God is really like. So what do we see?

First of all, we do not see a kingdom where dominion means exploitative domination. Mary is not Jesus' slave. He doesn't chide her for being lazy, telling her to get to work to serve him. Instead, he says that she, the one who simply sits at his feet and listens, has chosen the "better part" (Luke 10:42). Here Jesus presents a kingdom in which gazing lovingly at God is a preferred way of life. This is not to say that work is bad or unimportant. It is to say that in relationship to both God and God's created world, we are called primarily into a deep reflection on spiritual teaching before we act. Thus in our relationships with the natural world, we are called to exhibit the same reflective care and concern that Mary showed to Jesus and he, to her.

Secondly, it was in and through the normal events of the natural world that Jesus revealed "God's glory" (John 11:4). Housecleaning, illness, and death were venues in which Jesus taught Mary and others about his own nature as well as the power and promise of the gospel. His parables and teachings were of the natural world: wheat, mustard, pearls, and pigs (John 12:24; Matt. 13:31; Matt. 13:45; Luke 8:32). That fact does not imply these things *were* God but that through these things we can see and understand God.

Jesus didn't just talk to Mary about abstract theology. He raised her brother from the dead. This act occurred in nature; through the use of human flesh and blood, Jesus taught about a loving, gracious God. In the same way, our prayerful reflection upon nature can teach us much about how God desires us to work and live in the world.

Finally, Mary's relationship with Jesus was the antithesis of alienation. Mary even felt comfortable confronting Jesus about the death of her brother: "If you had been here, my brother would not have died" (John 11:32). Do we feel close enough to God to criticize God's actions? Jesus' sense of intimacy with this woman is equally powerful. Mary's tears move him deeply enough to weep, even though he perhaps knows the positive outcome of Lazarus's situation.

This picture of deep personal encounter, one that is mutual and felt by both human and God, is far removed from our own alienation with ourselves, our world, and God. In this scripture we come to understand God's vision for our relationship to all that surrounds us. Prayer practice in general helps us develop an intimate relationship with the divine; praying with nature is one specific way to draw away from self-imposed alienation and into the glorious reality of God shimmering around us.

ATTENDING TO OUR INTERCONNECTEDNESS

The intimacy with self, other, and God to which Jesus calls us (Luke 10:27) reveals a spiritual understanding of something that ecologists have been in the process of confirming for the last one hundred years: every speck of life on this planet is interconnected. As I sit and write I occasionally glance at a tree standing in my backyard. I am amazed to think that the oxygen I breathe in this minute may have been produced by that tree a few moments ago. I am able to breath, because the plants around me also are breathing.

Every day the reality of our global interconnectedness becomes more apparent—whether it's gas prices, the weather, the ripe strawberries from Chile in the grocery store in January, or the sound of various accents when we call for assistance with a sick computer. These signs bring home the reality that God created all and wove all into a single fabric that ultimately will be saved or lost together.

This profound truth is often missed by the highly individualistic Christianity of the West. Just as sin spread throughout nature to touch all creation, so too salvation spreads through all of creation to redeem this same fallen world. When God promised Abraham that his people would be a blessing to all the families of the earth (Gen. 12:3), God was expressing the desire for all creation to be redeemed, not just one part of it. Mary couldn't really be happy sitting at the feet of Jesus, knowing that her brother was dead. Having Jesus to herself couldn't be satisfying when one she felt so close to was dead and cut off from her. In the same way, we in our own individual churches cannot really rest happily with our own salvation when so many others suffer and are lost.

Thus spiritual leadership requires paying attention to the reality of our interconnected world, not in a superficial way but in a deep, profound way, a way so strong that Jesus weeps when we do. This process begins with our own attention to and prayer with all that God has created.

When I was studying clinical psychology, one of my teachers gave our class some advice. He said, "If you ever go into a therapist's office and see a dead or dying plant, turn around and walk out." At first we were all a bit stunned and confused by this statement. What did dead plants have to do with clinical psychology? The professor's point was that if a psychotherapist, supposedly capable of helping someone by attention to personal issues and problems, wasn't even paying attention to this living thing in his or her office, then that therapist was in no position to pay attention to you. Today I would offer the same advice not only about therapists but also about pastors and churches.

Prayer with nature gets you paying attention to the world around you. It draws you out of your self-centered head and into a God-centered world. Thus you start to pray with nature by paying attention to your own connections with creation. Ask yourself: *How do I eat? Do I look at sunsets? Do I pay attention to how I use energy? What really is the nature of my relationships with the world?*

These are profound questions. The fact that people often ignore them signals our lack of connection to God's creation and thus to God. Our failure to recognize these questions as spiritual questions reveals how we have ceased to take seriously the charge to have dominion over the created world. When I replace a wasteful incandescent lightbulb with an efficient compact fluorescent one, somewhere out in the world less energy is drawn from a power plant. This in turn makes it less necessary to build other plants, which in turn may allow a river to continue to flow freely or a mountain not to be mined out of existence.

The question for you as a leader who prays with nature is: *Do we know, deeply know, the reality of these relationships, and does this knowledge inform our knowledge of God?* The deeper your prayer life, the more the answer to this question is in the affirmative, and thus the more you are able to guide others into this intimate relationship.

PRAYER WITH NATURE can take many specific forms (see appendix), including caring for a plant in your office! Regardless of which form you choose, as you devote time and energy to this prayer, you begin seeing God all around you, and you become grateful for that which God has given. These are the fruits of praying with nature, which you then bring into the life of your community.

CHURCH LIFE AND PRAYER WITH NATURE

A community that prays with the natural world is a grateful community, and a grateful community is giving and compassionate. Unfortunately many churches exude an attitude of scarcity and stinginess. Contemplation with nature offers a wonderful remedy for this problem.

Consider the following story. A man goes out into the woods one day to cut down some trees. This is a normal enough activity, and we take for granted that we can harvest trees for lumber to provide shelter, furniture, and paper, some of the most important necessities of our lives.

However, on the day this man goes out to cut wood, something different happens. Just as he prepares to put the chain saw to the tree, a voice from the sky booms out around him, "That will be one billion dollars please." The man, in terror, drops the saw and looks around for the source of the voice. Finding no one, he tries to cut the tree again, but once again the voice cries out, asking for a billion dollars. This time the man replies, "Who is that?"

"God," says the voice.

"What do you mean, you want a billion dollars for the tree?"

"I've decided to charge for trees," replies God.

"Well, that seems a bit overpriced," says the man. "I mean, there are trees all over the place, and a billion for one seems like too much."

"Yes," says God, "there are trees all over the place, but can you make them?"

"No."

"Well then, I have a monopoly on the market, and I can charge whatever I want."

What if God charged us for everything we now get for free from God? Obviously we would all die. We couldn't function. It is amazing what God gives to us out of the natural world, all for nothing. Deep appreciation of this truth causes gratitude to well up in us, and as we become more grateful, we become more inclined to respond to ourselves, others, and our communities with generosity.

Thus, as a leader, it is helpful to promote prayer with the natural world. As with an individual, this prayer can take many forms. One excellent group with whom to initiate this prayer is the building committee or similar group that is in charge of the church facility. Since your building

is the community's environment, nature prayer will cultivate gratitude and hospitality within your church.
Encourage this body to begin the same practice of attention that you engage in.

What are the nature and condition of the church building, and how can repairs and changes to the structure be
done in a way that fosters the good kingdom of God?
Recently my church installed a new roof on part of the
building and new lights in the sanctuary. In both these
projects the people responsible focused on designs and
materials that would promote energy savings. As a result,
we now consume one quarter the energy we previously
used lighting the sanctuary and about one quarter less
energy heating and cooling the space. This not only makes
good economic sense but also raises awareness of our interconnectedness to all creation.

Another place to introduce reflective prayer with
nature into the life of the congregation or organization is
worship. You may have noticed the preference for nature
images in PowerPoint presentations shown in worship.
These images, designed either for intentional focus or for
attractive backgrounds, encourage people to pray with natural beauty. Worship leaders can become even more intentional about using the natural world as part of worship.
The elements of worship can prepare the way for people to
see God in all creation.

Finally, it is possible to provide opportunities for members of the community to experience prayer in nature
through retreats, outdoor activities, and camps. As with
all the practices in this book, approach the creation of
these experiences with an attitude of prayer rather than a

programmatic mind set that says, "We need to do this because prayer with nature is good."

The people who were with Mary saw her rise and go out, and they followed her. Soon they once again witnessed her at the feet of Jesus (John 11:32). This seems to be the posture Mary, a spiritual leader, adopts repeatedly. Sometimes she is listening with rapt attention, joyful to be hearing the words of Jesus. Sometimes she is weeping for the suffering of her brother and all who suffer, seemingly without God. Either way, she moves outside herself to bring her full attention to Jesus and seek a powerful relationship with the One who is the source of her life.

This is what we do when we seek God through prayer with the natural world. And as communities seek to pray in a similar fashion, they too find themselves in close proximity to the One who created us all, sustains us all, and saves us all.

ELEVEN

PRAYER AND LIFE IN THE WORLD

The Rubber Meets the Road

TRAVELING COMPANION
Jesus

[Jesus] called the twelve and began to send them out two by two, and gave them authority over the unclean spirits. He ordered them to take nothing for their journey except a staff; no bread, no bag, no money in their belts; but to wear sandals and not to put on two tunics. He said to them, "Wherever you enter a house, stay there until you leave the place. If any place will not welcome you and they refuse to hear you, as you leave, shake off the dust that is on your feet as a testimony against them." So they went out and proclaimed that all should repent. They cast out many demons, and anointed with oil many who were sick and cured them.

—*Mark 6:7-13*

*C*hurches and other religious organizations exist within the context of our fallen world. As we have seen, the practice of prayer and spiritual leadership has led us out of ourselves and into this world. We have moved from our hearts and minds into our bodies, which then move through time and space and in turn interact with the rest of the created reality. These practices, done in community, form groups of people into organizations that are living entities witnessing to the kingdom of God in our midst. Such communities have a life in the world that reflects their nature and the processes forming them.

I opened this book with the assertion that churches, in their manner and style of functioning, have largely become secular organizations. Consequently leaders in these organizations also have come to function in a secular manner when it comes to administration. If secular processes form the organization, then the life of the organization will be that of secular community. But what if the administration is done in the light of the Spirit? These final chapters address this possibility. What does it mean to practice contemplative administration? What does a community on its way to becoming a living spiritual entity look like?

How Did Jesus Run His Organization?

To reflect upon contemplative administration and seek to understand the prayer practices that build spiritual community, it seems reasonable to ask: how did Jesus run his organization on earth, and what did this organization look like? We claim that Jesus is ruler of the kingdom of God. He is the head administrator. So what is his style? How does he organize? How does he manage his people, and what organizational practices does he administer?

The early church confused the Roman Empire. Why? The early church didn't look anything like a familiar religious organization. It didn't have temples or church buildings; it didn't have priests; it didn't even have a codified set of scriptures. These early communities that looked to the risen Christ as their leader continued in this open manner for almost three hundred years after Jesus' death. Their style of organization mimicked the way Jesus had run his organization when he walked the earth.

Jesus' organization was loose and fluid; the most prominent characteristic of the organization was that it didn't have one! No wonder the Romans were puzzled and the chief priests felt threatened. Rather than devote most of his time to administering an organization as our secular world understands it, Jesus spent his time revealing the kingdom of God from within the situations he encountered. If he needed to feed people, he created a food program (John 6:1-14); if healing was needed, any place could become a clinic (Mark 6:53-56); if teaching was necessary, the world was the classroom (Matt. 5); finally, if a parade was required, a colt or a donkey could be borrowed (Matt. 21:2). And just as quickly, all these "organizations" could disappear when they were no longer necessary. Even the great temple might, in theory, be destroyed and rebuilt in three days (John 2:19)! We might call Jesus' administrative style minimalist at best and a type A person's nightmare at worst.

The passage quoted at the beginning of the chapter particularly reflects Jesus' poor sense of planning and lack of attention to detail. He sends his disciples out with nothing, telling them that somehow they will manage to find food, shelter, money, and proper work to do. Contrast this approach to the reality of today's world of permission slips, packing lists, insurance cards, liability waivers, and detailed schedules describing how every minute of time will be spent during an event.

I have already referred to the spiritual life as countercultural or, to use more biblical language, "not of this world" (John 18:36, KJV). Once again, in both the nature of the Jesus organization and his style of administration we see this otherworldly nature. What is so different about Jesus' approach to organizing his community? Of course, relationship to God is the first and most obvious answer, but what is it about that relationship that enabled Jesus to function as he did? Jesus summed up the answer when he said, "Do not worry about tomorrow" (Matt. 6:34).

Worldly organizations spend most of their time and energy worrying about tomorrow. This worry is manifested in strategic planning, financial predictions, five-year goals, and vision statements, to name just a few things. Not only do we spend huge amounts of energy on such activities, but, and this is the key point, we take these activities very seriously. So seriously that I often feel I can hear the trees of the forest cry out every time another organization sets out to write a strategic plan, for they know many of their fellow trees will die to make the reams of paper that will comprise such a document.

Jesus, on the other hand, knew that God would lead and guide him in his life and work. The path of his activity would be laid out for him day by day, week by week, and there really was no need to worry about tomorrow. This was especially true because for him, and therefore for us who claim to be the church, his vision statement was simple and clear: follow God.

THE CONTEMPLATIVE ADMINISTRATOR

Of course, it is impossible for anyone in the world to live and work exactly as Jesus did. You must do some planning, visioning, and thinking about tomorrow. But by examining what Jesus did and what the early church and many other spiritual communities since then have done, you can come up with some ideas and directions about how to lead from the perspective of contemplative administration.

First, a church organization must manifest the unique and different—countercultural—nature of the kingdom of God. As with all other practices, spiritual leaders must begin by reflecting this different nature in their own lives. How do you relate to your career, your material possessions, your family, your time and energy? Is there anything in these relationships that reflects the loving, nonanxious presence of the risen Christ? And what about your relationship with tomorrow? Are you anxious about it, or are you at peace with the reality that God will provide as you move into the unknown of the future?

From this examination of yourself and your own life move into reflection upon your relationship with the organization or part of the organization you administer. *What is my basic stance in regard to this organization? Am I open and at peace, being led by the Spirit, or anxious and afraid? Does concern about the unknown of the future drive me to micromanage or control everything that happens?*

The story of Jesus and the jar of ointment (Matt. 26:6-13) beautifully illustrates these contrasting stances relative to an organization. Jesus and the woman sit peacefully and gracefully, sharing a moment of intimacy and beauty. Meanwhile the other disciples are angry, anxious, and upset. Shouldn't the ointment have been sold to get money for the poor? What about our mission statement? Why are you being wasteful? In their distress the disciples leave the present moment and miss the tremendous teaching taking place. Their anxiety pulls them away from Jesus and what he is doing; it makes them concerned only with themselves and their own vision of reality.

A similar phenomenon happens in the church all the time. In countless arguments about how to spend money, how this or that should be decorated, why this person isn't showing up for such and such a function, or why the lights were left on in the narthex, we forget about Jesus. We don't see him at all. Contemplative administration is about keeping our eyes fixed on Christ. This is our only care and concern. We truly understand that heaven and earth can pass away, but the word of the Lord stands forever (Isa. 40:8).

CONTEMPLATIVE COMMUNITY

What practices, beyond the prayers described in previous chapters, can aid the contemplative administrator and the community who wish to follow Jesus and be formed in the light of the kingdom of God? I'll describe three. The first two are tithing and what I call the IMPOSSIBLE PROJECT (see appendix). The third is the practice of moving beyond agreement to loving your enemy. I am convinced this third is perhaps the most important community practice for our current era.

Tithing

TITHING is the ancient biblical practice of giving one tenth your gross earnings, your harvest, to God (see, for example, 2 Chron. 31:1-10). I intentionally specify gross earnings because in the Bible, the part of the harvest God received was the firstfruits (see 2 Chron. 31:5). People were to give to God first, just as God gives our life to us first, before we do anything with it. Unfortunately today people often give to God last, out of net earnings, whatever is left over after taxes, the mortgage, the credit card payments, and so forth.

Money is a difficult topic in the church, and frequently it is a difficult issue for spiritual leaders in their personal lives. When I was in seminary, a woman from the denominational pension board came to the school to offer a workshop on financial planning for ministers. Out of curiosity I decided to attend. I was both stunned and horrified that she spent the first half of an all-day workshop discussing how to balance a checkbook. At the break I asked her if she thought that this group of people, with an average age of thirty-six, really needed to spend three hours discussing balancing their checkbook. Her one-word answer: "Absolutely."

This shocking response suggests that spiritual leaders have unconsciously decided that paying attention to money and learning how money works don't qualify as part of their spiritual calling. I believe nothing is further from the truth. Because money is one of the great idols of our time, it is vital for spiritual leaders to understand how to deal with money, both your own and that of your organizations. You need the ability to teach yourself and others how to be freed from bondage to this idol.

The practice of tithing forces you to pay attention to your funds and your spending habits; it also forces you into a greater reliance upon God. Tithing encourages you to follow the example of Jesus and his organization, in which apparently people who followed him gave up most, if not all, their worldly possessions.

The Impossible Project

The impossible project encourages people to engage with the world in a new way that reflects the reality of the kingdom of God. It also brings together many of the practices discussed so far, including the practice of attending to money. In this day and age, many churches are closing their doors. Surprisingly perhaps, most of these churches die with a lot of money in the bank. These unspent funds are then moved to a denominational account where they again sit, usually unspent, until that time when perhaps the whole denomination dies.

The phenomenon of churches dying with money in the bank reflects the reality that the church was not really a contemplative community following Jesus or being led by a contemplative administrator. Why do I make this strong statement? Because a church that dies with money in the bank is a church that lived in fear and ran itself as a secular organization. It is a church that said, "We can't spend that money because then we might not have any." Or, "We can't spend that money because someone left it to fund a program that no longer exists." This church stopped listening for Jesus' call to ministry in their place and their time.

On the other hand, a church and church leaders who pray into the mission God gives them are always hearing the call of God to ministry in their community. Furthermore, the call they are hearing often summons them to do something impossible, to take the risk of faith that so many of our spiritual ancestors have taken before us (see Heb. 11).

The impossible project as a practice encourages you as a leader to ask questions about this calling for your church: *What are the desires in ministry that excite us? Is anyone in the congregation having dreams about what our church might be or do? Are there any outrageous ideas that have been voiced and then dismissed?* Attend to these questions, respond to them, follow the answers you receive; these activities lie at the heart of this practice.

When leaders and a faith community begin to live in the world of the impossible, a world inhabited by a God for whom nothing is impossible (Luke 1:37), they truly begin to see the miraculous happen. They allow themselves to step into the life of grace offered within a kingdom defined by boundless generosity and infinite blessing. They spend their money only to have it return a hundredfold (Matt. 13:8); they give only to receive (Luke 6:38); they know the life abundant offered by Jesus is real and in their midst.

Loving the Enemy

Disagreement and conflict in the church are nothing new. Paul's letters all appear to have been written in response to issues of conflict and crisis within certain church communities. In our day and age, we again face divisive issues within our faith communities. When such problems arise, humans typically default to seeking agreement; if that is not possible, we try to force "agreement" within an organization. In this way we lift "agreement" to the highest level of good, the gold standard for judging peaceful resolution.

Whether a tribe, an empire, or any number of other worldly organizations, defaulting to the goal of agreement characterizes those who seek resolution based upon adherence to the rules of the group. Typically we love people based upon whether they are our friends and agree with us. However, Jesus pointed to another way. He dared to make the radical claim that the hallmark of the kingdom was not people who all agreed but people who loved their enemies, the people with whom they did not agree (Matt. 5:44).

Loving our enemies is a powerful prayer practice, and it is one we must recover in today's environment of increasingly hostile, violent, and divisive disagreement. It is a prayer practice because it requires us to move outside ourselves into the space that is God. To insist that everyone around me agree with me once again makes my self, my ideas, my tribe, into God. On the other hand, to truly love my enemy means I see others as God sees them, other fallen yet beloved creatures who bear God's image. Spiritual leaders who seek to become contemplative administrators begin this process in their own lives and then encourage their communities to live the same way.

When people seek to understand acts of violence committed by one person against another, they realize that violence against the enemy usually is preceded by a process of dehumanization. The enemy is cast not as a person but as a subhuman or even a demon. Once this shift takes place, it is easy to hurt, exclude, or even kill those so defined. If you want to hear this process of dehumanization in action, turn on the radio or scan blogs on the Internet. Groups on the left and the right brand each other with labels and catchphrases meant to classify the other side not as people but as hateful caricatures.

The practice of loving your enemy, the prayer of loving your enemy, proceeds along the opposite trajectory: humanizing the enemy. The story of the good Samaritan is the story of both these processes (Luke 10:25-37). The people who pass the beaten man see him only as the labeled enemy, the thing that cannot be touched. The man who assists the injured person sees him not as a thing but as a fellow human being in need of help.

Pastors and other church leaders are told that their job description is to "love people." Behind this statement may lie the implication that official leaders are the only ones who are doing the loving so that everyone else can go on not loving. I have witnessed many church leaders suffer abuse in the name of loving "their sheep" while the abusive sheep are never called to accountability.

From the perspective of the spiritual life, this "loving the flock" job description while partially true is also fatally flawed. Parishioners aren't sheep—cute but mindless animals whose idea of a good time can be running off a cliff. Christian communities are composed of human beings called to love one another. A community does not hire a professional "lover" in order to be absolved of that task. As spiritual leaders pray into the love of enemy, they also must call their community to love in the same manner. You can do this as you answer questions such as: *Do I teach loving the enemy? Do I point to the common humanity of all people in the church? Do I focus on people's behavior toward each other rather than on arguments about issues? Do I try to encourage others to avoid labels and dehumanizing catchphrases?*

Looking again at Jesus' organization, we see a group of people who gave away their money, took on the task of changing a fallen world into the kingdom of God, and shouldn't have eaten with one another (Luke 15:2), touched one another (Mark 1:41), or cared for one another (Luke 8:2). Jesus engaged in these practices, and they are the practices of an organization that lives a new and different life in a broken world. As communities tithe, take on the impossible tasks, and love enemies, they too live into the promise of this kingdom. Leaders who live this life abundant (see 1 Tim. 1:14, KJV), are also following the One who lived a life as radical and disturbing as it was loving and grace-filled.

TWELVE

A PRAYING COMMUNITY
Growth in Spiritual Leadership

TRAVELING COMPANIONS
The Early Church

*You will receive power when the Holy Spirit has come
upon you; and you will be my witnesses
in Jerusalem, in all Judea and Samaria,
and to the ends of the earth.*

—*Acts 1:8*

*All of them were filled with the Holy Spirit
and began to speak in other languages,
as the Spirit gave them ability.*

—*Acts 2:4*

*J*esus didn't appear to agree with the notion that leaders are born and not made. According to the book of Acts, the group of approximately 120 people who gathered to pray and wait for the Holy Spirit were instantly changed into spiritual leaders who began to take the new faith to the whole world. The church began as a community of praying followers who then became a community of pray-ers leading as they themselves were led by the Spirit.

This final chapter will explore this issue of ever-expanding leadership within the praying community. The chapter does not describe a specific prayer practice so much as it describes signs that a community is praying together and engaging in spiritual leadership. Furthermore, these signs are not uniform; nor should they be taken as prescriptive because the nature and form of ever-expanding leadership will be unique in each time and place as God enculturates the living gospel in a community.

Micromanaging Leadership

In the historical denominations, clergy leadership is a highly organized and micromanaged affair. Candidates for leadership are grilled by committees, take required courses, pass mandatory ordination exams, and are then certified as ready to take a call. Like so much beef stamped with the USDA seal of approval, these leaders go out into the world now worthy to spread the good news.

Although ordination committees talk a lot about being "led by God," it is often hard to see how the Spirit can work its way in between the forms and the tests, the rules, and the "right answers." Meanwhile many churches wait for months or years for pastors. The creation of a professional clergy class conveys the message that no one at the church can really handle the job of ministry. Thus when there is no pastor, the community dwindles and sinks into liturgical depression. No wonder church becomes a spectator sport—ironically a development often lamented by pastors!

If the stories of Acts and Paul's letters provide any guide, God certainly didn't work this way when the church was being founded. Jesus ascends to heaven and simply lets the group of followers know that from this point on, they will be spreading the gospel (Acts 1:6-11). He appears to be perfectly comfortable with this arrangement, and seems to have the utmost confidence in his followers in spite of their lack of training. Several hundred years after the first Pentecost, leaders of the early monastic movement appear to have acted out of the same sort of confidence. Anyone who led a disciplined life of prayer and devotion, they believed, would be able to take on the mind of Christ, be led by the Spirit, and could then aid others in this endeavor.

As the church lost this spirit-filled confidence in the people of God, it created rigid communities led by the rule of law and the absolute power of the leader. This micromanaging by church leadership disempowered the laity and spawned an extreme dependence upon pastors and other church leaders.

When I first arrived at our current church, I was asked to make decisions about some of the most mundane things: the location of the coffeepot during coffee hour, whether or not to put a note on the bulletin board. At first I thought these questions were polite jokes, but I was wrong. They were deadly serious. Even more crippling was the evident lack of spiritual confidence and sensibility. People were panic-stricken if I asked them to pray grace at a group meal or at a committee meeting. That was supposed to be my job—they "couldn't" pray out loud.

I began to realize that this dependence on professional leadership and the resulting disconnection from God were not the fault of the members of the church but rather of the church at large. The church had essentially communicated that laypeople weren't qualified enough to lead in a church setting—either with regard to basic functional decisions or in spiritual matters. This message not only is not biblical but it has had negative consequences for church communities: their pulpits go unfilled at the same time the laity feel unable and unprepared to lead.

Now this is not to say training is unimportant or accountability is unimportant. I do mean to say that a community bathed in prayer is a community where God is continually forming leaders. People have difficulty realizing this truth, experiencing Pentecost's power, because today's church defines a leader as someone capable of running programs and standing up front in worship.

From the perspective of spiritual leadership, these are skills that some leaders may have, but those skills really have little to do with leadership per se. Spiritual leadership is simply the sharing of the presence of God as that presence is experienced, noticed, and named—a process that occurs through the prayer life of the leader. This is what Paul meant when he wrote, "I have been crucified with Christ; and it is no longer I who live, but it is Christ who lives in me" (Gal. 2:19-20). As Christ lives in you, he leads and guides you in whatever way is appropriate for your state of being. As this occurs you become a spiritual leader.

SIGNS OF GROWTH IN COMMUNITY SPIRITUAL LEADERSHIP

So what indicates that a community is growing collectively in spiritual leadership? If you are a leader looking around your community, how do you recognize the Spirit moving in ever-wider circles of grace? In these final pages, I want to reflect upon eight ways to notice fruits of a community prayer practice that is birthing spiritual leaders. All these signs were evident in the early church as described in the Bible, and they are ones that continue to unfold in communities that pray together in a deep and consistent manner. Because these signs reveal God in your midst, they all interact and overlap, reinforcing the understanding that the risen Christ is indeed alive and present in your community.

Open Space

The practice of prayer creates open space—space in our hearts and minds, space in our lives, space in which God can hem us in (Ps. 139:5), space in which we can notice and listen for the activity of the divine in our lives. Open space is a commodity in short supply in the secular world and often in the church. Thus one sign of a growth in spiritual leadership in a community is a greater sense of space. People aren't running in and out of meetings as fast as possible; the procession of activities on Sunday morning has a greater sense of openness and relaxation; decisions don't have to be made instantly.

If we look at the early church in Acts, we see a sense of spaciousness in the early communities. "Day by day, as they spent much time together in the temple" (Acts 2:46) depicts a community that isn't in a hurry, isn't frantic. People who engage in prayer practices naturally begin to slow down and look around them, see and appreciate their community and those in it. They become curious about one another and about God. They also have the space to begin to notice how God is working in them; their desire to follow these leadings grows. Once again, leadership arises out of the space of "nothingness."

Decrease in Anxiety

Closely related to this sense of space is a general decrease in anxiety. Our hurried and harried lives have generated a tremendous increase in our individual and collective level of anxiety. This is no less true in the church than anywhere else. People in my current church at first found it revolutionary that I wasn't distressed when we needed to adjust something in worship on short notice. We have all unconsciously come to believe that God needs us to function at peak efficiency and perfection; otherwise, perhaps the universe will dissolve.

A community that prays together begins to understand, deeply, the meaning of the statement "Remember, I am with you always, to the end of the age" (Matt. 28:20). We really do have nothing to fear, nothing to be anxious about if Christ indeed lives in us. Paul, whose life in the early church certainly wasn't smooth or free of uncertainty, reflected on a life free from existential anxiety when he wrote, "If God is for us, who is against us?" (Rom. 8:31). People today long for, crave, the peace that comes from being free of constant worry. As members of the community relax into the presence of God, they become conveyors of this peace. This kind of leadership has nothing to do with activity or skills. People naturally are drawn to individuals and groups who seem able to live lives according to the promise of God's salvation. And these individuals and groups become leaders by the very nature of their being.

Empowerment

Low anxiety gives rise to the next sign of community leadership, high confidence—or empowerment. People who begin to encounter God in their lives are empowered by this creative God who forms the universe and enables them to take the gospel into the world. A church staff engaged in the life of prayer can help facilitate this process by which all in the community gain spiritual strength. As their anxiety decreases, as more space is created, God can enter into the lives of all who connect with the church.

People I meet in church circles express amazement on hearing that our church never uses pulpit supply. When I am not available for a Sunday service, members of the congregation do the entire service, including the message. When we first began this practice, many were scared and horrified. Some, who have since spoken in church, insisted they could never do it. However, this practice has resulted in tremendous increase in the faith, confidence, and empowerment of our community. As people have gotten up and shared of themselves and their lives, others have been able to see God's action in a "regular" person, not just in stories told by a professional. This powerful practice of leadership has encouraged many to go on and use their God-given gifts in other areas of their lives.

Certainly this aspect of leadership development is particularly obvious in the book of Acts. As the Holy Spirit moved out into the community, more and more people arose as leaders in the early church. These people became empowered to do amazing things. Furthermore, the community validated that these gifts were of God as they witnessed them building up the community.

Increased Trust in God

This action of God to empower and raise up leaders gives birth to the next sign of a praying community: a great increase in trust in God. I have mentioned that many problems in the church at large, especially around the issue of leadership, stem from our lack of trust that God is with us and among us. However, as our prayer life brings God out of the shadows of our consciousness and into the full light of our lives, we begin to trust in God's immanence.

This trust emboldens members of the community to step out into the world as spiritual leaders in a way they never considered possible before. They are willing to give new things a try, willing to say yes when asked to do something. They find new faith to overcome obstacles. Trust in God comes forth as the community experiences God in their midst as a real "person" who is indeed trustworthy.

Again the example of the early church is instructive. It seems to me that the actions taken by the people we read about in scripture—adventures, imprisonments, leaving old traditions for something new, even to the point of risking death—none of these would have been possible without trusting God. And although our situations today may be much less extreme, it takes the courage created by a deep trust for someone to step out of his or her comfort zone and lead others in a faith activity. Yet, like people in the early church, we too will see such activity erupt as the Holy Spirit moves through our life together.

Invitation

The next sign of the presence of God at work developing leadership in a praying community is invitation, itself an attribute of the Holy Spirit. Just as Jesus invited the disciples to follow him, so too God invites us into a life with God; and, therefore, a community living a life of prayer manifests the spirit of invitation. A wonderful illustration of the connection between receiving the gospel and invitation is the story of Paul and Lydia in Acts 16. Once Lydia receives the gospel from Paul and Silas and has been baptized, she responds by inviting them to her house.

In many ways, leadership and invitation are synonymous. Leaders invite others to share in the wonderful thing they have found—Jesus. In looking for signs of spiritual leadership, it is important to distinguish between an invitation loaded with worry over numbers and success and an invitation derived from the joy of finding God. The great contemplatives were often indifferent as to whether anyone ever joined them in their prayer life. The gift of God is such a reward in itself that another's presence is not required to validate the gift. At the same time, God places in humans the desire to invite others to share in this wonderful bounty, and people do so with a spirit of joy and excitement that can be contagious.

As you look around your community, ask whether you are inviting others in, especially "the least" (Matt. 25:40) of our social order. You will find as your practice of prayer grows that your community will change and grow in its ability to welcome others, especially those who are different or unknown.

Generosity

The preceding signs of God's presence and of spiritual leadership all add up to a community that is generous. In the creation God has given us, in the salvation God offers us, we come to understand that God is immensely generous. In the same way, a community that comes to know this bounty through their own experience of prayer, is a community that leads in generosity.

This generosity can occur in many ways: generosity of spirit, of time, of money, of sharing gifts. Whatever the form, spiritual leaders give generously of all that God has given to them. In the New Testament we hear about people who gave of everything in order for the new community called the church to become a living reality. If a people following God are praying and discerning God's will for that community, the spirit of generosity will provide for everything that community needs. Like the other signs of leadership, the generosity of members in the community will inspire others to follow in their footsteps.

"Yes" to Change

Numerous comments, jokes, dark stories, and general discussions circulate about the issue of change in the church. Most point to the fact that church communities, especially traditional ones, tend to see change as a bad thing. Every church leader I've met is familiar with the expression "We've always done it that way." Yet scripture describes a set of communities that lived, worked, and struggled with the dynamic change inherent in the work of the Holy Spirit bringing new life to a fallen world. Change was the norm rather than the hated exception.

In fact, this reality of change is true of our lives in general. The only thing constant in our world is change. Every moment differs from the last; every instant brings something new; this is the action of a creating God, as Jeremiah tells us: "The LORD has created a new thing on the earth" (Jer. 31:22). Churches seek to avoid this reality and resist change in part because of a disconnection from God. One great sign of God at work in the hearts and minds of a praying people, then, is that fear of change evaporates. The typical default to "No" when a need to change presents itself disappears. The community starts from the perspective of saying yes to the work of God as discerned in their midst and therefore yes to wherever God leads.

This yes arising out of the depths of prayer forms and inspires leadership. Because we begin to hear the living Word in this affirmation at the center of our lives, we are able to lead others into and through the changes in our life together. Energy is released and used, not stifled and held back. We become comfortable with the movements of the Spirit, and we are able to embrace these movements because they indeed give us life and joy. As these qualities emerge, so too do leaders.

Fun

This brings us to our final indicator of the presence of spiritual leadership. I used to have a T-shirt imprinted with the saying *Are we having fun yet?* I wore it so much that I no longer have that shirt, although I wish I did. *Are we having fun yet?* This is a great question for the church. In what may be the earliest book of the New Testament, and thus one birthed directly out of the earliest church,

Paul tells us, "Rejoice always" (1Thess. 5:16). Are we having fun yet?

Unfortunately in church the answer is no way too often. That no signals a community not following in the path of prayer, the path of the Spirit. Too often church is sour and depressed, as are church leaders. Or, if leaders aren't depressed, then perhaps they are taking themselves far too seriously. Either way, there is often precious little fun to go around.

Spiritual communities create people who do rejoice. They rejoice in the Lord; they rejoice in themselves; they rejoice in one another. They appreciate laughter and mirth; they understand that God has a sense of humor. In a country that consumes millions of mood-altering pills a day, those who can laugh again in the midst of life are indeed leaders; and such people appear with wonderful regularity in a community that prays.

Looking back over these signs in a praying community, you may notice I have said nothing about growth, about new programs, about missions, about particular activities of any kind. This is intentional. Organizations that create spiritual leaders will create missional and evangelical activities. However, the programmatic work is not the primary goal of the spiritual life nor the primary aim of spiritual leadership.

I make these assertions for one very simple reason: salvation is not a program. Salvation is an alteration in our being as we come into relationship with God. Therefore the signs described above point, however indirectly, to the presence of salvation in the midst of God's people. They point to the presence of Jesus.

So I invite you to take the journey of prayer. Not merely as a solitary pray-er but as a spiritual leader, one who guides and encourages others along a path of peace and glory. Follow Christ, and as you do, ask him to form you into one who also fishes for people. For the spiritual life is way too precious to keep to ourselves but rather is a banquet to be shared.

Let us pray.

APPENDIX

A Step-by-Step Guide to the Prayer Practices

Under each chapter heading you will find instructions for doing the featured prayer practice as an individual or in a group.

1 LEADING FROM THE SILENCE

Solitude and silence are the basis for most practices described in the book. Here are general tips and guidelines to help you become comfortable with these cornerstones of contemplation.

For an Individual

- Begin the practice by noting your intention to spend more time in solitude and silence. All the practices in the book begin with such an act of intention: We make a positive statement to ourselves and to God that we desire a deeper awareness and experience of the divine.

- Begin to notice times when you are already in solitude and/or silence—when you take a walk, when you are in the car alone, when you are at home by yourself, when you go to the gym to work out.

- During these times, consciously bring to mind your intention to pray. Ask God to help you notice the presence of Jesus in your life. Address God with any specific questions or concerns you might have about your spiritual life.

ᐒ Listen for the reply from God. Don't be concerned if nothing happens. Continue to bring your mind back to God in the silence.

ᐒ Over time, pay attention to your desires around your prayer life. Perhaps you find yourself wanting to pray more. Perhaps you find your life changing in various ways. If you find yourself desiring more silence and solitude, respond to these desires. Go on a retreat, take up some of the other practices in the book, spend more time alone with God.

For a Group

ᐒ First the group makes a commitment to spend more time in silence together. This commitment could be made during an opening prayer time or as part of a structured activity.

ᐒ The group chooses or the leader suggests how to create times of solitude and silence for the members. After such times, the group debriefs together. For example, group members might go for a fifteen-minute walk, spend time praying silently in the sanctuary, or practice another silent prayer practice alone.

ᐒ The group gathers to share experiences of solitude and silence. Everyone is invited to talk without trying to fix one another's problems or reinterpret others' personal experiences. The group leader needs to have enough experience with solitude to be able to offer constructive feedback if it seems necessary.

ᐒ Group members pray for one another as a means of supporting their spiritual journey. They may pray for God to give them strength for moving into deeper solitude and silence.

2 Praying the Bible: Entering the World of Scripture

Lectio divina, or "divine reading," is a powerful way to encounter God in scripture and offers a wonderful practice for either individuals or groups. The individual practice has four phases. The group practice can be adapted to fit the setting; here I describe a three-phase group practice.

For an Individual

Phase 1, *Lectio* (reading/listening)

- Choose a passage of scripture. Although any passage will do, a psalm, a story about Jesus, or one of the poetic passages from a prophet works very well. For example, try Mark 1:14-20 or Isaiah 40:1-5.
- Read the passage to yourself twice. Don't be caught by the literal meaning of the scripture. Rather, listen for the word or phrase that catches your attention.
- Silently focus on that word or phrase. Repeat it a few times. Allow it to sift through your heart and mind.

Phase 2, *Meditatio*

- As you continue to focus on your word or phrase, pay attention to the thoughts and feelings it evokes.
- What images, what thoughts, what memories come to mind?
- Continue to ask God to speak to you through this word, and continue to listen for the reply.

Phase 3, *Oratio*

- At some point you may find yourself wanting to reply to God. What desires has your prayer awakened in you?
- You may have found an area of your life that needs some work.

- You may find you are grateful for something and you wish to express that gratitude.

- You may feel called to a new course of action in your life.

- Whatever you sense, do not rush the prayer. Continue to wait and listen as God forms your prayer and desire in your heart.

- Speak your prayer of desire, longing, or action to God. Continue to listen in the silence.

PHASE 4, *Contemplatio*

- In this final phase of the prayer, the conversation with God draws to a close. Having heard a word from God and having expressed your response to that word, you now allow yourself to rest in the silence.

- Allow your mind to settle.

- When you feel that the prayer has come to an end, express your gratitude to God. This can be as simple as saying "Thank you" or "Amen."

For a Group

This process closely follows the individual process, adding at the end of each phase an invitation to the group members to speak the results of their prayer.

PHASE 1

- The group leader reads a Bible passage aloud twice.

- In the silence each person begins to listen for the word or phrase in the passage that speaks to him or her.

- After a period of silence, the group leader invites the group to share aloud each person's word or phrase. (People are to speak only their word, not a commentary on its importance to them.)

PHASE 2

- ✑ The group leader reads the passage aloud again.

- ✑ This time, the group leader invites participants to wait for an image, thought, or phrase that arises in response to the passage.

- ✑ After another time of silence, the leader invites group members to share what they received in the silence.

PHASE 3

- ✑ The leader reads the passage a third time.

- ✑ The group members are invited to listen for how God is speaking to them through the passage.

- ✑ After a time of silence, group members are invited to share what they have heard in this phase of the prayer.

PHASE 4

- ✑ After everyone finishes sharing, the group could close the time of prayer with an expression of gratitude: a brief verbal prayer or a moment of silence.

- ✑ In the group process, it is important that group members not comment on one another's observations but simply listen during the sharing period.

3 NO OTHER GODS: CONTEMPLATIVE CONCENTRATION AND THE JESUS PRAYER

For an Individual

- ✑ Decide how long you wish to spend in prayer. At first you might try fifteen minutes. You may want to spend more time as the prayer becomes familiar.

- The Jesus Prayer can be done anywhere—as you take a walk, in your office, on the bus, late at night in bed, in a church.
- Repeat, in your mind, *Jesus Christ, Son of God, have mercy on me.*
- The repetition should be continuous; that is, the phrase is to be silently repeated again and again.
- Allow the words to flow into your entire being.
- When you have finished your time of prayer, express your thanks to God.

For a Group

- The leader establishes or the group decides on a set amount of time to do the prayer.
- The group may wander as space permits; members may choose a place to pray individually or the group may decide on a location.
- Group members individually practice the prayer as described above.
- When the group gathers again, each member has an opportunity to share his or her experience. The purpose of this time is not to fix one another's problems or determine who did the prayer "correctly."
- The group leader needs to be prepared to give encouragement and support to group members who feel they "don't get it."
- Group members can encourage one another to try the prayer on their own.

4 SILENT CONTEMPLATIVE PRAYER:
BE STILL AND KNOW

Apophatic prayer is the simplest prayer and perhaps the most difficult. It is helpful to do this prayer more than once, as the experience of the prayer on any given occasion can be good or bad, and
either is perfectly correct.

For an Individual

- Decide on a length of time for the prayer, usually twenty
  to forty-five minutes. A shorter time may be preferable
  for beginners.

- Pick a word to use as a point of focus during the prayer.
  It doesn't matter what word you choose as long as it
  reminds you of God's presence.

- Find a quiet place to sit. It is helpful to sit in a good
  upright posture, with your hands resting on your thighs.
  Generally this prayer is done with eyes closed. If that is
  uncomfortable, then allow your gaze to rest on the floor
  six to eight feet in front of you.

- Begin your prayer by silently saying your word once.
  Then just sit quietly. Unlike the practice of the Jesus
  Prayer, you need not repeat the word continuously.

- When you notice that you have become distracted by
  your thoughts, silently repeat your word to bring yourself
  back to the present.

- When your time of prayer has ended, express your gratitude to God.

For a Group

- Select a comfortable space for your prayer time. Arrange
  the seating so people are not facing one another. Decide
  how long the group will pray.

- One person begins and ends the time of prayer. A small bell or chime may be used to signal the beginning and ending.
- The leader starts by saying, "Let us pray."
- Group members then do the practice as described above for the set period of time.
- The leader ends the time of prayer by reciting the Lord's Prayer.
- Some group discussion following the prayer is valuable. During this conversation, the leader can assure people that they are not doing the prayer "incorrectly" and encourage them to return to their word during the prayer when they become distracted.

5 Examining Spirits: Doing the Will of God

For an Individual

- Choose a period of time to examine in prayer. This can be a day, a week, or a specific event.
- Allow your mind to wander through that period of time. Some questions you might ask yourself about that period include:

What are you most/least grateful for during that time?
When did you feel a sense of love, peace, joy, life (the gifts of the Spirit)?
When did you feel exhausted, dead, drained, angry, mean?
What specific events, thoughts, or experiences draw your attention?
What aspects of that time repel you?
What moments speak to you of your deepest desires?
What things feel out of place, uninteresting?

Ask yourself, *When did I notice God during this time? What felt like a time of God's absence?*

☙ As some answers to these questions arise, notice what they suggest to you about the future. How is God calling you into being? Toward what actions, activities, or attributes is God drawing you?

☙ Repeat this prayer at regular intervals in order to see how God is working in your life.

For a Group

A group may do the examen in two ways: (1) Each individual in the group does an examen and shares the results with the others; (2) the group applies the examen to an activity or a time that group members experienced in common.

Method 1

☙ Each group member receives the instructions for an individual provided above and then takes a period of time, decided by the group or leader, to do the examen.

☙ When that time is up, the group members share their experiences. The group serves as a place for support, affirmation, and feedback for each individual.

Method 2

☙ The group that gathers to do the examen has participated in some common activity, such as a worship service, a planning process, an outing, a mission activity.

☙ The group does the examen on this common activity. Each member of the group takes time to pray over the activity, using the individual steps above.

☙ Then the group shares the results of their prayer. This provides an opportunity to see the many ways God is working in the common activity. It also gives the group a chance to see things that are "not of God."

Ê The group will use these reflections to guide its future activities.

6 To Create Is to Pray: Creativity and the Divine

For Individuals

Ê Begin by noting your intention to notice God through your creative actions. Notice what activities you already do that involve creativity. Also notice any desires for creative activity that you do not currently do. These could include but are certainly not limited to:

Decorating your house or room
Getting dressed
Art in school or other settings
Cooking
Your ministry or other job
The activities you and your friends participate in
Writing projects

Ê As you do these activities, bring to them an attitude of prayer. Ask God to help you seek Jesus during your time of creativity.

Ê Notice what happens during these prayer times.

Ê Give thanks to God.

For a Group

Ê The group leader selects a creative activity, usually some form of artwork.

Ê Make sure plenty of art supplies are available.

Ê Members of the group pray creatively for a set amount of time. They may leave the group meeting place or all work in the same area. The point is not to make a finished piece of art but rather to use the creative time as an opportunity to converse with God.

    ☙ When the time is over, the group gathers together and shares observations about the creative experience.

COMBINING CREATIVITY WITH OTHER PRAYERS

For either an individual or a group, creative practice may be combined with other prayers. For example, you might spend time drawing after a *lectio* prayer or after the examen. Or get out art supplies after taking a walk in silence and see what happens. There are many possibilities. Combining creative prayer with another practice works particularly well in a retreat setting.

7 SPEAKING AND WRITING: THE WORD AND OUR WORDS

Basic Journaling

This practice can be done either by an individual or in a group setting. Simply take time to allow yourself to write about your thoughts, your desires, your questions in relation to God. Pray to God on paper. Watch over time as your relationship with Jesus deepens and grows. In the group setting, these observations and reflections can be shared as a means of support.

Conversation with God

This writing practice can be done alone or in a group setting.

    ☙ Express your desire to have a conversation with God.

    ☙ Draw a line down the center of a piece of paper.

    ☙ The left side is for your words; the right side is for God. You are the scribe for both of you.

    ☙ Begin the conversation with your side. Write down your thoughts, questions, concerns, or anything on your mind.

- Listen for any replies. Write down whatever seems appropriate on the right side of the page. As strange as this sounds, you may be surprised at the results of this prayer!
- In the group setting, share your conversation with others.

Wall of Prayer

This is a group journaling or creative prayer project.

- You will need a fairly large table and a long piece of butcher paper.
- Lay the paper out on the table. Place paints, markers, pens, and other art supplies all over the paper so that they are accessible to people standing around the table.
- Gather the group around the table and provide a beginning point for the prayer: a topic, a piece of scripture, or a question.
- People begin to write and draw their prayers in response to the starting point.
- After ten minutes or so, everyone moves to a different place on the paper and begins to work again.
- When the time for prayer is over, hang the paper on a wall so all can see the the group's prayers.

8   INCARNATING PRAYER: THE BODY AND THE SPIRITUAL LIFE

Breath Prayer

This prayer can be done as an individual or in a group setting.

- Designate a length of time to pray. This prayer can be done in almost any setting—while walking, sitting, or lying down.

- Note your intention to experience God through your body. Ask God to make you aware of the presence of the Spirit in your breath.

- Draw your attention to your breathing. Try to breathe from your diaphragm, letting your abdomen rise and fall easily. Don't force your breath or breathe too quickly.

- Whenever your thoughts wander, bring your attention back to your breath. Pay attention to the breath of life filling your body.

- When the time of prayer is over, notice your feelings and the state of your mind. Thank God for this experience.

- If in the group setting, members may share experiences.

Body Sculpture

This group prayer practice can be described as a physical *lectio divina*.

- Find a room with an open area where group members can create the body sculptures. The leader selects a passage of scripture and then reads the passage aloud twice.

- The leader reads a single word from the passage. The word should be read twice.

- In the silence that follows, members of the group, as they feel called to do so, go to the open area and form a sculpture with their body in response to the word. They hold their posture.

- After it seems that all who wish to create a sculpture have done so, the leader again reads the word. This signals all to return to their seats.

- Repeat this process for several different words in the scripture passage.

- Afterward, share your experience of the prayer with one another. Combining this practice with a creative art activity works well.

9 Walking toward God: The Journey Made Visible

Slow Walk

This practice is appropriate for both individual and group prayer.

- ❧ Set a length of time for the prayer—at least fifteen minutes. If you are doing the prayer in a group, designate a route for your walk. This can be a circle in a room or another configuration outside.
- ❧ Begin with an intention to listen for God with your whole being as you move through space.
- ❧ Start walking slowly. With each step, slow your pace further. Eventually try to take one step every fifteen to thirty seconds (this will feel extremely slow).
- ❧ Pay attention to your breath, your body, your heart, your mind. When you become distracted, focus on the sensation of your feet contacting the floor with each step.
- ❧ At the end of the prayer, give thanks to God.
- ❧ In the group setting, reflect together on the practice.

Labyrinth

These first instructions apply to both individuals and groups. Following are additional notes for a group practice.

- ❧ Find a labyrinth. There may be one at a church or retreat center in your community. The difficulty of locating a labyrinth can be the biggest obstacle to this practice.
- ❧ There are three phases to the practice: the walk in, resting at the center, and the walk out.
- ❧ Walking into the labyrinth is a time for shedding anything that keeps you from communion with God. You may want to silently repeat a scripture as you journey. Or use the time to notice your thoughts and feelings and consider these questions:

What is it like to be on this journey?
Is there anything I need to let go of?
Is there something blocking me from experiencing God's love?
Am I in need of forgiveness?
Do I need to forgive?

- ❧ The center of the labyrinth is seen as the point of unity with God, the symbolic dwelling place of God. When you arrive at the center, simply rest in God. Remain there as long as you like. Converse with God in whatever way seems appropriate to you.

- ❧ The walk out of the labyrinth is the process of bringing God back out into the world with you. As you retrace your steps, continue your prayer and conversation with the divine.

- ❧ In what new way might Jesus accompany you into the world?

- ❧ What are your thoughts and feelings as you contemplate going back out into your life?

- ❧ Do you come with any new insights, experiences, or plans?

- ❧ When you finally leave the labyrinth, give thanks to God for your time there.

ADDITIONAL INSTRUCTIONS FOR A GROUP

When entering the labyrinth make sure to allow space between individuals as they enter. You can post a person at the entrance to signal each person when to enter the labyrinth.

- ❧ Feel free to pass others along the path. Everyone proceeds at his or her own pace in the labyrinth.

- ❧ Watch the other people as they walk. Notice that you are all journeying to God as the body of Christ.

- ❧ After walking the labyrinth, take time to share feelings and observations about the prayer.

10 Praying in Nature: Contemplation, Creation, and Leadership

General Prayer with the Natural World

This prayer is similar in form to the general prayer of solitude and the general prayer of creativity. In this prayer, you simply begin to turn your attention to God when you find yourself in natural settings. In addition you can intentionally plan to spend time in nature to be with God. This prayer can be done alone or in a group.

- Make known to God your intention to listen for God's presence in nature.
- Then as you encounter a natural setting (while hiking or walking, gazing at a sunset or sunrise, seeing the moon at night, catching a glimpse of an animal or a beautiful flower), bring your attention to God.
- Notice your thoughts and feelings.
- Notice the amazing beauty of creation.
- Become aware of the power of the natural world.
- Reflect upon the gift of your own life.
- Thank God for the time of prayer.
- In a group setting, take some time to share your experiences.

Combining Other Prayers with Natural Settings

As with creative prayer, prayer in nature may be combined with other practices. Next time you are in a beautiful place, pray the Jesus Prayer or do an examen. Take photographs for use in a worship service. Use the power of God's presence in the natural world to help you with your other prayer practices.

Deep examination of natural item.

This variation of the general prayer in nature works well in a group or retreat setting.

- ✑ Select a natural item for use in the prayer practice—a flower, a blade of grass, a rock, anything that catches your eye.

- ✑ Choose a specific length of time for the prayer. In the group setting, the leader may set the length. Anywhere from fifteen to thirty minutes is appropriate.

- ✑ Follow the instructions for the general prayer in nature listed above, focusing your prayer and your attention on the single item.

- ✑ Pray deeply into this one tiny piece of the created world.

- ✑ How is God speaking to you?

- ✑ At the end of your prayer time, you might want to journal about your experience or engage in creative prayer in response to what you have heard.

- ✑ In the group setting take some time to share reflections with one another.

11 Prayer and Life in the World: The Rubber Meets the Road

Tithing

The aim of this prayer practice is to begin to try to give away 10 percent of your gross income. You may give that money to a church, or you may give to any group doing the works of justice and peace. As Jesus says in the parable, "When you do it to the least of these, you are doing it to me" (Matt. 25:40, paraphrased). It is important that you feel good about the church or other group to which you give the money; you need to believe that this group is working to manifest the kingdom of God. That feeling is different from feeling that the work of the group benefits you, which it does not have to do necessarily.

Then the practice is simple: Give away your money—or at least try. Watch what happens as you attempt to do this. This practice will affect all aspects of your life, so it presents an opportunity to converse with God about many things: how you spend your time, how you spend your money, what is really important in your life.

The Impossible Project

This practice is most appropriate for a group that will be together for a while, such as a church group.

- Begin to pray together about the work that God is calling the group to do. The group might begin to do the examen on its mission.

- As time goes on, notice what longings and desires arise in the group. What is "tugging" on the group? What is God pushing the group to do and be in the world?

- After a while some specific suggestions may surface. Keep track of these. Don't discard any idea. Pay attention to which suggestions excite the group. Do the examen on a list of suggestions.

- Finally, one or two ideas may grab the imagination of the entire group. In all likelihood these ideas will seem impossible—the projects too large, too expensive, too outlandish.

- Pick one of the projects and try to do it.

- Most importantly, as you proceed, continue to remain in prayer about the project. Because it is impossible, it is God's project, not yours; if you cease to pray, you will fail.

12: A Praying Community: Growth in Spiritual Leadership

As I mentioned in the chapter, there is no specific set of instructions for this practice. Listed below are attributes that I feel must be part of a praying community. For a description of these attributes, see the chapter:

- ✑ Humility
- ✑ Obedience to God
- ✑ Empowerment of each community member by God
- ✑ Prayer, both individual and group spiritual practices
- ✑ Scripture
- ✑ Relationships among community members characterized by the following attributes:

  Treating one another as you would treat Jesus

  Caring for one another

  Serving one another

  Being hospitable

  Honesty

  Trust

- ✑ Community discipline that focuses on appropriate consequences for actions and honest appraisal of behavior
- ✑ Leadership characterized by spiritual teaching
- ✑ Stability—finding a way to consistently practice these attributes as a community over time
- ✑ Some form of community work/service
- ✑ Some form of community poverty

A Retreat Model

There are many ways to do a prayer retreat, but all of them amount to the same thing: Take time to pray! What I offer here is a general outline for what a daylong prayer retreat might look like in a group setting. A few variations follow as well as notes about elements that could be added or deleted. The outline can be tailored to fit whatever time frame you have available (I have done prayer "retreats" that are one hour long!). If you are doing the retreat on your own, simply omit any of the group activities.

OUTLINE

Early morning: Prayerful worship as a group.

Breakfast

Morning: Teach and do a prayer practice.

Lunch

Afternoon:
- Offer some free time.
- Teach and do another prayer practice, or repeat the same prayer practice you learned in the morning.
- Time for group reflection and sharing.

Supper

Evening: Prayerful worship

Possible additions
- Consider adding silence to all or part of the day.
- Add a talk on prayer or a scriptural meditation.

- Consider adding fasting as part of the retreat. Caution is in order regarding this decision. Special dietary needs or eating disorders may affect group members, so evaluate the situation before incorporating.
- Add a group reflection time in the morning.
- Offer individual spiritual direction as part of the retreat time.
- If you are in a beautiful setting, encourage people to take walks.
- If possible, add group work tasks as part of the retreat. Simple tasks like meal preparation or just setting the table may be found in the kitchen or dining hall.
- Use a single passage of Scripture as the theme for the whole retreat time.
- Create another type of theme to ground the retreat.

Above all, when on retreat, have a wonderful, relaxing time with God!

ABOUT THE AUTHOR

DANIEL WOLPERT worked as a psychologist and spiritual director, a farmer, a teacher, and a construction worker before earning his graduate degree at San Francisco Theological Seminary. Over the past eighteen years he has taught adults and youth and led retreats in such settings as the Art of Spiritual Direction Program at San Francisco Theological Seminary, the Youth Ministry and Spirituality Project, and Sabbath Retreats. Daniel now serves as a church pastor in Crookston, Minnesota, where he lives with his wife, Dr. Debra Bell, and their two sons, Sam and Max.

THE SOUL OF TOMORROW'S CHURCH:
WEAVING SPIRITUAL PRACTICES IN MINISTRY TOGETHER
by Kent Ira Groff

SPIRITUAL PREPARATION FOR CHRISTIAN LEADERSHIP
by E. Glenn Hinson

Available from your local bookstore
or direct from The Upper Room
1-800-972-0433
www.upperroom.org/bookstore